WRITING Extraordinary ESSAYS

Every Middle Schooler Can!

David Lee Finkle

SCHOLASTIC

NEW YORK • TORONTO • LONDON • AUCKLAND • SYDNEY
MEXICO CITY • NEW DELHI • HONG KONG • BUENOS AIRES

Dedication

For Andrea, the real Mrs. Fitz:

Outside validation is sweetest because it validates your faith in me!

Cover design by Brian La Rossa
Cover photo © Blend Images Photography/Veer
Interior design by Solas
Interior comics by David Lee Finkle

ISBN-13: 978-0-545-05898-8
ISBN-10: 0-545-05898-8

1 2 3 4 5 6 7 8 9 10   40   13 12 11 10 09 08

Contents

Acknowledgments

This book has had many people helping it along the way.

First, this book is really a tale of two newspapers. Thanks to Ronald Williamson and Nick Klasne at the Daytona Beach *News-Journal* for taking a chance on a local cartoonist in 2000 and making a lifelong dream come true. I'm on the comics page! And thanks to Mike Lafferty at the *Orlando Sentinel* for first agreeing to publish the essay that got the ball rolling.

Thanks also to . . .

My editor, Gloria Pipkin, for discovering me online and hunting me down. Writing this book has been the best professional development I've ever had.

My family, Andrea, Christopher, and Alexandra, for their patience with my preoccupied demeanor as I juggled this book, a daily comic strip, and teaching.

My wonderful principal, Mamie Oatis, who was supportive from the get-go, and the wonderful faculty and staff at Southwestern Middle School—but especially to Dr. Patty Arnold and Susan Tyree who helped me get my Wikispace online and running smoothly. And thanks to my students for teaching me how to teach—I'm still learning—and for always giving me fresh material! Special thanks to Katherine Beckwith.

Introduction

This book began as an essay I wrote for the *Orlando Sentinel* about standardized writing tests—in particular the Florida Comprehensive Achievement Test (FCAT) writing assessment that my students take each February. But that essay began with a student. This student (I'll call her Cathy) had been in my eighth-grade language arts class, a star writer in a class of excellent writers. I had really thrown myself into teaching essay writing to these students. I'd gotten them to go beyond the old five-paragraph formula, to start sounding like "real" writers. That had been my mantra: I want you to sound like published essay writers, not like students writing for a test. That class succeeded on the test beyond anything I might have hoped for. Most of the class got 5's or 6's, the highest scores possible. But what made it particularly sweet was that we had done it not by teaching (and learning) to the test but by learning how real essayists write.

Cathy had moved on to a different school for ninth grade, but I would see her occasionally and ask her how things were going—in particular, how she liked high school English. Cathy shook her head, and said, "The teacher gave us a packet about how to write a good five-paragraph essay."

I asked some colleagues why this kind of writing instruction might be going on in freshman English. Their reply: passing the FCAT writing assessment was a graduation requirement. (This changed in 2008.) The schools were pushing for everyone to pass. Not to excel, mind you, to *pass*.

I had worked hard to get that class of writers to think outside the five-paragraph essay box, and now Cathy was being told to climb back inside. I decided I should write about this dilemma for the "My Word" opinion section of our newspaper. I wrote it in front of the class for my then-current eighth graders, and e-mailed it to the paper.

I heard nothing for almost two weeks. But then I received an e-mail: the column had been sent to Mike Lafferty, an editor and columnist who had spoken to my classes on occasion. He'd decided to print it. Rather than paraphrase it, I'll simply print the essay here as it appeared in the newspaper.

Last May when my school's FCAT writing scores arrived, my principal hand-delivered them to my room. I accepted them with a shaky hand. As the Language Arts Chair at my middle school, I wanted us to do well. We did. A huge percentage of our students passed the test. Even better, many received the highest scores of 5 and 6, which are very difficult to get.

My excitement over our scores dipped, however, when I discovered that high scores don't really matter to the state—or our school grade. All that matters is the percentage of students meeting the minimum standard.

The minimum standard of 3.5 out of 6 is, quite frankly, not a stellar example of writing. Paragraphs often begin with gripping phrases such as, "my second reason is," and the essay will sometimes end with a thought-provoking, Forrest Gump–esque, "that's all I have to say about that."

The 3.5 minimum score is all that matters, though, and that fact directly impacts instruction. If high scores don't matter, why shoot for them? Just get everyone to a 3.5 and you're done. You can achieve this goal by teaching a formulaic, five-paragraph essay: a main idea and three supporting details (in no particular order). Tell 'em what you're going to tell 'em, tell 'em, and then tell 'em what you told 'em. This Formula for writing an essay may be a fine survival tool for some students, but for many bright, enthusiastic student writers, it's a cage.

Taking students to a score of 5 or 6 is riskier. You chuck the Formula. You read published essays together to drink in the sound of good writing. You delve into organization patterns and logical arguments. Content dictates form, so essays may be any number of paragraphs, depending on what the writer has to say. You teach about the "showing" detail and the catchy turn of phrase. You teach them that writing is about having enthusiasm, about being engaged in the world and interested in what's going on around you.

In fact, you teach them about real writing, not about the FCAT.

Such an approach isn't "safe." Some teachers still preach that you can't even "pass" the FCAT writing unless you write precisely five paragraphs. My scores belie that idea. A vast majority of my own eighth-grade language arts students got 5.5's or 6's last year—without the formula.

On Tuesday my students will face the FCAT writing. Although the state doesn't seem to value excellence, I can still tell them their excellence has value where it really matters: the real world. I don't want to see them someday writing five-paragraph "My Word" essays that conclude, "And that's all I have to say about that."

A few days after my essay went to press, I received an e-mail from Gloria Pipkin, editor of an online standardized-test-reform newsletter called F-TREND. She had included a link to my essay in F-TREND and wanted to talk to me about a book proposal.

So here I am writing a book. I only had about 500 words for the essay, so having about 45,000 to use for the book is quite freeing.

This book is about having it both ways. Your students can earn not just passing scores but **high** writing scores. More importantly, you can get them to transcend the test itself. You can teach them how to be great essay writers. This book is not about teaching to the test, but teaching beyond the test. Shoot for a minimum score, and you may get it, but your students haven't really learned anything about how real writers work. Shoot for great writing, and test scores get pulled along for the ride without much extra effort.

The strategies I'm offering here are usable in any kind of classroom: a full-blown writing workshop or a more traditional classroom. Take them and make them your own.

One further note: in addition to teaching full-time, I draw a comic strip, "Mr. Fitz," that appears on the "Coffee Break" page of the Daytona Beach *News-Journal* five days a week. "Mr. Fitz" is, amazingly enough, about a middle school language arts teacher. These comic strips appear throughout the pages of this book because the strips often illustrate points I'm trying to make about writing, about students, about teachers—and about standardized testing. I don't refer to the FCAT directly in the strips, as I would someday like to go nationwide with it. My wife and I invented a fictitious standardized test to use in the strip: the Universal SKills, UNderstanding, and Knowledge test. The U-SKUNK. You will see references to that throughout the book as well. Mr. Fitz, the character, is my alter ego, of course—but he's not me. Sometimes he's a better teacher than I, but sometimes he makes mistakes I would never make, simply because mistakes often make a point and get a laugh better than doing things right the first time.

CHAPTER 1

Read a Genre to Write a Genre

I'm beginning this book about essay writing by talking about poetry . . . and comic strips. I'm beginning this way because certain things about writing hold true for any kind of writing, be it poetry, comic strips . . . or essays.

Over the years I have had the dialogue shown in the comic strip above with any number of students in my class or at Young Authors Conferences I have attended as either a teacher or a guest speaker. These students were all showing me their overstuffed notebooks of poetry, but virtually none of them read poems with any regularity. They write poetry regularly, having almost no grasp of the traditions they are writing in, or the myriad tools and subgenres at their disposal.

I politely advise them to start reading poetry. Not every poet uses the same tools and techniques, but there is a lot to be learned from actually reading in the genre you are asked to write in. Of course we often ask students to write poetry without ever asking them to read real poetry. How many of the ubiquitous "poetry project" packets are out there in classrooms, teaching students that poetry is as simple as filling in the blanks?

Another story, another genre—this one about comic strips. As I mentioned in the introduction, I write a daily comic strip for the Daytona Beach *News-Journal* called "Mr. Fitz." Since I like to draw comic strips myself, I also run an after-school Cartooning Club. What has interested me year after year is how many student cartoonists want to draw comic strips, but, like the poets, never actually read the funnies. They throw themselves into drawing comic strips, without ever having really studied the features of the form.

This failure to read the genre you are trying to write baffles me not only with comic strips and poetry, but with other genres as well—especially with essays.

FILL-IN-THE-BLANKS ESSAYS

Most middle school language arts teachers are being asked to focus on essay writing these days, mostly because of state writing tests. The irony of the current climate in middle schools is this: Many schools attempt to ensure that their students pass state standardized writing tests by teaching them formulaic writing styles that actually hamper them from excelling as writers—or as test takers. They teach students to "fill in the blanks," just like the poetry packets. They don't teach students to read real published essays and then emulate them; they teach them simple formulas that they think will make all students pass the test. And many of the formulas we give to students have nothing to do with real essay writing.

Here is my short list of erroneous things we teachers often teach about essays:

1. An essay must have five paragraphs.

2. An introduction must state the main idea of the essay and the three supporting reasons.

3. The conclusion must do the same things as the introduction.

4. Every supporting or "body" paragraph must have a topic sentence and "x" number of supporting sentences.

5. Supporting sentences must use good descriptive adjectives.

6. You must choose from a list of transition words (e.g., *then, next, first, second, third*) to go from one paragraph to another.

There are more erroneous things we teach, of course, but these are the big ones. But if we look at what real essay writers do, we find that they don't follow any of these rules. I have students come to me in middle school who have been drilled with the formula, told they will not pass the class without the formula, and, most importantly, told they cannot pass the standardized test without the formula. I have read books on how to get students to pass these tests, and many of them simply reiterate the five-paragraph essay Formula.

Eventually, when they really start writing for the real world, or for a teacher who doesn't promote the Formula, they will, as Yoda says, need to "unlearn what they have learned."

In the meantime, many students grow to hate essay writing. They find it dull, uncreative, and, well, formulaic. And they tend to write boring, standardized, monotonous essays.

The Essay as Art Form

Students need to be introduced to the essay as its own unique—and in its own way, creative—art form. Before they can write good essays themselves, they need to read some essays that they actually like and want to emulate. Often, all we provide them with are sample essays from the state test to score and compare to their own papers. Students need to read examples of "real" published essays—but even that is not enough. They need to analyze the techniques published essayists use, and then apply them in their own writing. This is trickier than it sounds, but well worth the effort.

I'll hit on another genre again. Most people take comic strips for granted, assuming there isn't much to writing them. Sometimes I feel that way, until I actually try to teach the kids everything that goes into creating one. Writing a comic strip involves coming up with a humorous idea and deciding how to present it in some combination of words and pictures, how to create an ironic twist that will make the reader laugh, and how to organize the miniature story into a series of frames. A cartoonist must also decide how to stage each frame of the story in terms of balancing dialogue and artwork—for example, staging the characters so that the character to the left usually speaks first. He must decide how much time is passing between frames and when to throw in a "timing" frame that involves a character thinking or giving the audience a "look." A comic strip looks simple, but there is a lot going on in the simplest of strips. If you haven't read a lot of comic strips and analyzed what makes them work, it is very difficult to write one successfully.

Essays are at least as complicated as comic strips. There are a lot of writer's tools very specific to the essay form to learn and put into practice. In this book I'll attempt to do two things:

- Help you teach students to find, analyze, and learn from real essay writers
- Help you take the multitudinous tools real writers use and teach students to apply them to their own essays

There are many fringe benefits to encouraging students to emulate real writers. The least of these benefits is that students who go beyond the formula often go beyond the minimum passing score on standardized writing tests. But there is another, even more important benefit: **engaged** students.

If we focus exclusively on standardized writing tests, we tend to give students generic, bloodless, state-approved writing topics that never fully engage students' real interests. Students need to connect writing to their own lives. Too many students have the attitude Liz has in the following "Mr. Fitz" cartoon.

FINDING REAL MODELS

I frequently lament the fact that literature books don't have more, and better, examples of essay writing that students can actually emulate. Many textbook essays are too long or too short to be appropriate models. Some of the essays I've seen in eighth-grade literature books are almost essay fragments, while others are several pages long. Many real life situations and nearly all writing-test situations call for essays to be one or two pages long.

But length aside, the chief problem I've discovered with textbook essays is that kids think they are boring. Many of the essays, including pieces by excellent, world-renowned writers, are fine for adults but leave students cold. If we want kids to really like the essay genre and *want* to write in it, we need to find examples of essays they will buy into. They need to read essays that make them laugh or cry or get angry—essays that make them say, "Whoa! That was good writing." One of my students, after reading C. S. Lewis's essay "Meditation in a Toolshed" announced that she was "in love with" the author because she liked the essay so much. This infatuation quickly faded when she discovered Lewis had died in 1963.

So where do you find well-written essays that are relevant to students' lives and issues?

Magazines

One place to find well-written essays to share with the class is magazines. *Time* usually has an essay by a contributing columnist, as does *Newsweek*. *Newsweek* also features a "My Turn" column of 1,000 words contributed by a *Newsweek* reader. If I share one of these essays, I point out that *Newsweek* pays $1,000 for the essay—this usually impresses students.

Books

The essay is alive and well, thank you very much, and numerous books out there are packed with great short essays. Sometimes simply reading an essay aloud is enough to help students develop a love of the genre. That said, there are a lot of essays being written today that are simply inappropriate for middle school classrooms. *The Year's Best Essays* might seem like an obvious choice, but isn't necessarily. Many of the essays are inappropriate, and even more of them are too long to serve as good models.

So what books do I recommend? If you can find books of syndicated columnists, they work well, though you are in a way getting second-hand newspaper material. Anna Quindlen has several books of essays, including *Living Out Loud*. Some of the topics are from long-bygone eras of news, but often the issues are still relevant. Thomas Friedman's essays from *The World Is Flat* are usually short and focused, and are very much about current issues that we face as a society.

On the other hand, Dave Barry essays are not usually very relevant to current events, except in a smart-alecky way, but they are fun to read and demonstrate a wide range of writing tools. The best book to get is *The World According to Dave Barry*, which is actually a collection of three books of essays. There are a lot of gems there. Interestingly, humor essays can sometimes provoke diverse reactions. I've had some classes howl at Dave Barry's prose, some merely smirk politely, and some tell me that they just "didn't get it." That's okay. This reaction can turn into a discussion about humor. What makes something funny to us? What makes us laugh? What prior knowledge do we need to "get" a joke?

Robert Fulghum, who wrote the famous essay and book *All I Really Need to Know I Learned in Kindergarten*, has several books of very enjoyable, untitled essays, including *Maybe, Maybe Not;* and *Uh-Oh*. In his book *It Was on Fire When I Lay Down on It* is a great expository essay (untitled, so I call it the "MOTB—Mother of the Bride"). It blurs the lines between narrative and expository as it tells the story of a mother of the bride who goes way overboard trying to give her daughter the most elaborate wedding ever, only to have disaster, of a gross and hysterically funny nature, strike at the event itself. I will revisit that essay again over the course of this book. One of my favorite essays of all time, which I share just before the holidays each year, is from the same book. It tells the story of a failure named John Pierpont, only to reveal at the end that he is the author of a greatly loved song of winter.

There is currently a movement toward collections of essays by different authors and celebrities as well. Marlo Thomas has compiled two books of essays titled *The Right Words at the Right Time*. The first book contains essays by many different celebrities and public figures, all explaining (in expository essays) how they received just the right words at the right time at some juncture in their lives. Jay Leno writes about the children's book *Mike Mulligan and His Steam Shovel*. Whoopi Goldberg writes about advice her mother gave her. Rudy Giuliani writes about the words that got him through the week of September 11. Not only are these excellent models of expository writing, but many are also by people that students know as public figures. These people, most of whom are not "professional writers," know how to write well, and words matter to them. Students don't see their role models writing essays very often. Another, similar book edited by Charles Grodin is titled *If I Only Knew Then . . . : Learning From Our Mistakes* and again contains essays by many public figures and celebrities. There are many, many books of essays out there. Do a search for "essay collections" at Amazon.com or barnesandnoble.com and the list is endless. There is no need and no way for me to list them all. My point is this: don't limit yourself to what's in your textbook. And especially don't limit yourself to student samples from your state test. They have their place, which I will discuss later in the book, but I have seen teachers hold high-scoring student samples from the state test as the highest level of achievement for their students. "This is a '6'! Go for it!" We must be giving students other examples, published examples, of essays to emulate.

Newspapers

If looking through a lot of books seems overwhelming, there is another great source of essays that is constantly replenishing itself: newspapers, both in print and on the Web. Every day across the country, newspapers publish essays on up-to-date subjects in all areas of life: politics, current events, entertainment, sports, family life, and business, to name only a few. There are nationally syndicated columnists, but there are also many local columnists who write mainly about local issues—local sports, politics, and entertainment. Add to that the fact that many newspapers have guest editorials by everyday citizens who are not necessarily professional writers, and you have a plethora of possibilities.

If your school has a Newspaper in Education Program, so much the better. You may have access to free newspapers for your entire class at least once a week. If you want to look at one particular essay as a class, then the resource is available.

Adopt-a-Columnist

Adopt-a-columnist is a program I designed for my students to get them reading essays on a more regular basis, particularly essays on topics of interest to them. They read one essay per week, and then fill in a chart that analyzes it (see Figure 1.1). Here is the letter I send home to parents at the start of the project, which runs as long as I'm teaching essay writing in depth.

Dear Students and Families,

We often ask you students to write essays, but we don't spend nearly enough time asking you to read good essays so that you can get a "feel" for how they are written, how they sound, what kinds of tools professional writers have in their toolboxes. The irony is that there are dozens of good examples of essay writing being published every week in our newspapers and magazines.

This brings me to the ongoing homework project I am giving you for the next few weeks. I would like you to "adopt" a columnist. There are many of them to choose from, local and national. I would like them to meet the following criteria.

- The essayist/columnist must write at least once a week in his/her publication.
- The essays should be about a printed page in length.
- Each essay should generally be focused on one topic.
- The essays should be about political, cultural, and societal concerns. Sports, entertainment, and "lifestyle" columns are also allowed.

That's all there is to it.

You may find the essays in print form, online, in my classroom, or in the Media Center. You need to clip or print at least one essay a week and put it in your file folder. Then, complete the attached chart, listing the column headline and telling about the writer's tools the essayist used. That's all there is too it. I want you to read observantly and consistently to get a sense for how professional writers organize and develop their ideas, and how their organization, details, word choices, and sentence structures all contribute to the whole.

You will be reading a single columnist for four weeks, and then switch to a new writer. I will ask to see your progress each Friday, when we share essays in small groups and with the entire class. You may do more than one essay a week and you may also ask for additional forms.

Happy reading!

Mr. Finkle

P.S. I have no control over and am not endorsing the views or content of the essays students read, and I am not responsible for either. I am only asking students to consider the qualities of the writing itself for this assignment. Parents may wish to preview columns for appropriateness of topics.

ADOPT-A-COLUMNIST CHART	
Columnist	**Date/Title of Column**
Organization: List the main ideas of the essay, not necessarily for each paragraph	
Type of organization/transitions	
Details/Word Pictures: List or quote your three favorite specific details from this essay	
Sentence Flow: Copy one sentence you thought had a lot of "punch."	
Grabber and Clincher: What type of grabber and clincher did the author use? Were the grabber and clincher related?	
What worked for you? What didn't?	
Did you agree with the writer? Why or why not?	
Other comments?	

Figure 1.1

I tell students they don't have to agree with the columnist every time, and I encourage them to read outside their comfort zone. I've had some pretty vehemently political eighth graders over the years, and I think it does them good to read essays by people they don't necessarily agree with.

On Fridays, all students bring their columns and analyses to class. I organize students into groups, and students in each group share the essays they've found, telling why they liked or didn't like the particular essay. Any group that feels it has a particularly good essay can share with the class at large. By the end of the week, each student in the class has read and analyzed one essay on his or her own, heard three more essays in the small group, and then heard two to six more essays with the whole class. Most of these essays are about 500 words and don't take long to read. The small-group work takes 15–20 minutes, and the large-group sharing and discussion takes 10–20 minutes. This may seem like an odd use of one class a week, but the benefits are many.

Students often can't wait to come to class to share their essays. If it is a funny essay, they sometimes have to pass it to someone else to read because they can't get through it with a straight face. When the time comes to switch to a new columnist, many students don't want to leave their old one behind. I have to reassure them they can still read their "old" columnist just for fun.

Because there is choice involved, there is much more buy-in from students. For many students, it may be the first time they have ever read essays for pleasure—even for students who gulp down a new novel every two days. Another benefit is that students may start looking at the news in a new way. Many students are very aware of news from the world of pop culture: "[fill in the blank] is in rehab again!" They often do not keep up with news stories about real issues and real ideas. Adopt-a-columnist is a way to get students more interested in the world around them. You may even want to collaborate with your social studies teacher to make the program interdisciplinary! By the end of a nine-week grading period, students will have read nine essays on their own and heard 27 read in their groups. That's 36 essays, not counting the ones that get shared with the whole class.

A Word About Appropriateness

Even a family newspaper deals with touchy subjects sometimes, and what is fine for one student's family may be considered off-color by another's. Columns may deal with issues such as abortion, gay marriage, and binge drinking and rape on college campuses. As you may have noted in the letter above, I explain to my parents up front that I cannot predict in advance what the columns may be about, and I warn them that I am not endorsing any of the views of the columnists myself, merely using their work as models of published essay writing. I circulate during our small-group "column-shares" to monitor for any essays that might be a little "iffy" during the all-class sharing time. I have yet to have a parent or student complain, and students feel daring dealing with real-life, grown-up topics. I find this activity works a little better with older middle school students—older seventh graders and eighth graders.

STRATEGIES FOR READING LIKE A WRITER

"Reading like a writer" is a phrase that has been kicked around for a while now, but it can be hard to get kids to do it. How do you get students to read like writers? Well, it depends on what you are trying at the moment to teach them to do as writers. Almost any writing skill or technique can be analyzed in the context of existing essays. The idea is to train students to observe what real writers do in actual essays. The list of techniques and structures writers use is virtually endless. One problem with going with a set list of structures and techniques is that it may inhibit students. They should always be looking for more and interesting writing techniques and approaches to add to their toolboxes.

For starters, however, here are a few things students can look for in essays:

- How does the writer grab our attention?
- How much space, if any, does the writer devote to giving us background knowledge?
- How is the essay organized?
- How does the writer use transitions or create flow from one idea to the next?
- What kind of persuasive devices are used?
- What kinds of details get used?
- What phrases or words establish or develop the tone of the piece?
- Where are long, short, and medium sentences used for effect? Where are fragments used for effect?
- What word choices were particularly appropriate?
- How did the author conclude the paper?
- How do we know the author cares about the topic?

I usually do not overwhelm students with all of these questions at once, except for some kind of final exam in reading like a writer. Usually I target two to four items, either to introduce, practice, or review them. I use several variations on Cornell notes (see figures 1.2 and 1.3), also called two-column notes, but I will often add a third column. As students read an essay, they fill out the appropriate columns on the chart, depending on your focus.

Prewriting Tools

Many of the analysis tools I use in class are also useful as prewriting tools. I will discuss using them in that way in Chapter 3 on organization and Chapter 4 on prewriting.

TRIPLE COLUMN OUTLINE FOR ANALYZING ORGANIZATION AND DETAIL		
Column One Main ideas of essay/outline; type of organization	**Column Two** Details to support the idea	**Column Three** Types of details (metaphors, word pictures, etc.)

Figure 1.2

TRIPLE COLUMN OUTLINE FOR ANALYZING ORGANIZATION AND TRANSITIONS		
Column One Main ideas of essay/outline; type of organization	**Column Two** Transitional devices (words, phrases, etc.)	**Column Three** Relationship between paragraph topics (cause and effect, comparison and contrast, spatial, etc.)

Figure 1.3

Also, I sometimes use the "Adopt-a-Columnist" chart (see Figure 1.1), or one similar to it, to do an overall, rather than focused, analysis of an essay.

Students almost never mind analyzing an essay in this way. It is fast, instructive, and more interesting than the "questions" at the end of the text. I almost always include organization as the first column, simply because it provides good practice with the skill of outlining as well as a framework to add the other details they are observing.

Our Challenge

The idea of this chapter is to get beyond simple formulas for writing that have nothing to do with how real writers write. You want students to do the work here. Challenge them to find new techniques that you haven't even noticed or pointed out. Some organizational styles defy all our neat categories, yet they still produce organized essays.

I hesitate to bring it back to "the test," but many states, including mine, are now adding multiple-choice questions to their writing tests that ask students to analyze essays concerning their organization, details, and word choices. Teaching your students to read this way will reap benefits there as well. But the real reason to teach students to read like writers is that it makes them better readers as well as better writers. As we analyze essays, we discuss the techniques and structures the writers use and begin putting them into practice. Putting them into practice will be the focus for the rest of this book.

CHAPTER 2

Setting the Stage

Before we can get our students writing, they need to have something to write *about*. For some students, this is a huge problem. They may talk all day (often when they shouldn't), but when it comes time to write, they draw blanks. In a desperate attempt to fill in those blanks, we may give them writing prompts. I have done it myself. But I think there are better ways of dealing with students blanking out—what I call "writer's blank"—than simply handing them topics. As my editor mentioned to me in an e-mail, quoting John Dewey, there's a world of difference between "having to say something and having something to say."

THE PROBLEM WITH PROMPTS

Real writers write for real reasons about things that are important to them. They write because they want to change things, influence people, or express themselves. If we are constantly flooding our students with writing prompts like "Describe a special day/friend/teacher" and "Persuade your administration to take your point of view about gum/homework/vending machines/dress code," we are not teaching them to do what real writers do.

Many of the standardized topics we throw at students aren't bad, but when it is all we give them, they often give up on generating their own topics. Worse yet, they may forget how to come up with their own topics. Worst of all, they may disassociate writing from real-life relevance altogether.

When I ask students to come up with their own topics, I can tell how "far gone" they are by their responses:

The student who has not yet been crushed under the weight of standardized-test-like prompts will say, "I can write about *my own* topic! Great!"

The student who is partially crushed by generic prompts will say, "I don't know if I can think of anything!"

The student who has been completely smushed under the weight of Persuade the Principal to Take Your Point of View About Improving Cafeteria Food will say, "Please, please just *give* me a topic! I can't think of anything! I have nothing to say! Nothing interests me!" When you hear students saying things like this, the situation is critical.

But there is a cure to the ennui of the writing-blanked. It is to start, bit by bit, to have students delve into their own lives and the world around them for topics. This will make them better, more engaged writers, but more importantly, writing has the power to make any of us better, more engaged *humans*.

Tapping Into Students' Lives

Many of my students over the years have been writing-blanked. Some years it felt as if most of them were. I've had students tell me that nothing interests them, that they can't remember anything important that has ever happened to them, that they don't have anything that makes them angry. I never seemed to be able to reach some of these students. For whatever reason, they didn't want to tap into their own lives for material, or they simply didn't want to think about their own lives.

But for the most part, I've had success with getting students to realize they have plenty to say. What follows are some of the strategies I have used to get them to this realization.

Why Write?

Too often, I think, we tell students that they need to know how to do things because they will need those skills at some "later" time. You'll need to know this in high school. You'll need to know this for college. And, of course, the ever-popular "You will need to know this because it will be on the test." What about "You need to know this for real life"?

When I survey my students early in the year, most of them say they have received plenty of the "you'll need it for the test" advice, but very little, if any, of the "you'll need it to live your life" advice. I try to remedy this situation.

At the beginning of the school year I usually start with an activity called Why Write?

I write at the top of my board, "Why Write?" Students form groups, and I tell them it is each group's job to brainstorm as many real-life reasons to write as they possibly can. Every time I do this activity, I find we have trained them well, for when I ask for examples, many of them first call out, "For the state test!" and "So we can do well in high school." I quickly point out to them that these are academic reasons, not "real- life" purposes. I also point out that our definition of writing is "putting words together to create meaning." This means that typing things without using a pen counts as writing. Signing your name on a check does not.

(At this juncture, many students like to point out to me that I do much of my writing for school, so I must not live in the real world. I inform them that not having to live in the real world is one of the many fringe benefits of a career in teaching. They never know whether to take me seriously.)

Once they get the hang of it, though, when we've hit on five or six examples, and hands are reaching in the air for more, I tell them to work in their groups for ten minutes—which often turns out be 20–25 minutes—to come up with more real-life reasons to write.

I walk around to encourage them and drop an occasional hint. When time is up, I rotate around the room, one suggestion per group, till we run out of suggestions or time, whichever comes first. Usually we run out of time rather than reasons. Some of the reasons students have suggested are listed in Figure 2.1.

Examples of Real-Life Reasons to Write

résumés	flyers and brochures
job applications and cover letters	advertisements
love letters	instructions
eulogies	directions
thank-you notes	e-mails
scripts for videos at work	letters (business and friendly)
editorials/letters to the editor	excuses
letters of complaint	insurance narratives
business letters	toasts/speeches/tributes

Figure 2.1

Our lists are never the same, and never complete, but that's not the point. The point is that there are many, many real-life reasons to write that have nothing to do with school. Students keep this list at the front of their language arts notebooks, and we refer to it throughout the year. I tell them to remind me of it if I start talking about The Test too much.

Students need to know that they have plenty of opportunities to write outside the realm of tests. They also need to know that their writing, if it's done well, can affect and influence other people, and possibly even change the world around them. But once we have emphasized how many real-life reasons there are to write, we must once again delve into the question of what to write about.

Enthusiasm Map

Most students have special interests, but they often don't think of them as topics for writing. Often, they are also unaware of how the things they are interested in are connected to each other—hence, the idea of an Enthusiasm Map (see Figure 2.2). It is a kind of stream-of-consciousness way of brainstorming topics to write about.

I model it for students on the board or overhead before I have them do it. They usually dive in with, well, enthusiasm.

This is completely nonlinear. Students may follow one category all the way down to a very specific topic, or they may list several categories around their name from the start, and then develop them. Encourage them to look for connections between seemingly dissimilar enthusiasms. On my map, for example, I have connections between Cartooning and Movies, Group Games and Teaching, and "Peanuts" and Theology. The challenge is for them to come up with everything they can possibly think of that interests them, and then to see how their different interests relate.

When students know their enthusiasms, they can write about them all in different ways. They can explain why they like something, describe how to do something, persuade other people to like it, compare something they like to something else they like or hate, or write a narrative about it. They can even defend their enthusiasms when they come under attack. I once wrote a whole op-ed piece about the demise of traditional, hand-drawn animation in favor of computer animation, a phenomenon I heartily protest.

I ask my students to update their map periodically since they may be developing new interests. As a class, we delve into this list whenever they need an expository topic.

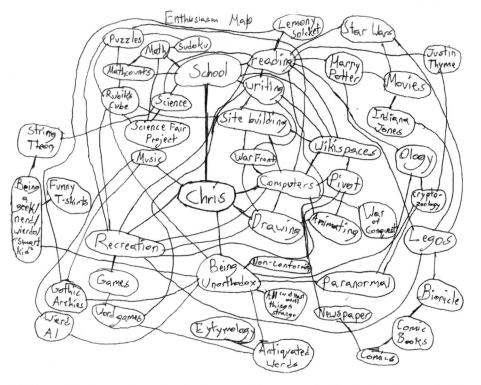

Figure 2.2 Have students start by writing their name at the center of a blank piece of paper that is turned sideways. Then have them draw lines out to major categories and then subcategories of interests.

Frustration Map

I have many quotes posted in my room, but one of my favorites is one that I found attributed to Lily Tomlin: "Language evolved out of man's deep inner need to complain." Listen to anyone long enough, including each of your students, and eventually you will hear him or her complain.

As a follow-up to the Enthusiasm Map, we create our Frustration Map (see Figure 2.3). This fun activity is very similar to the Enthusiasm Map—it's a kind of Non-Enthusiasm Map. It is a map of all the things that frustrate you or tick you off, but it also includes things that you simply think are wrong, wrong, wrong.

Again, students start by putting their names in the middle. And then they go to town. I usually suggest some categories to get them started, such as school, home, friends, and the United States and the world. I also tell students that they should list attitudes that bug them: snobbishness, laziness, or rudeness all count.

Students attack this assignment with relish—they usually start before I've even finished explaining it. It's a chance for them to vent. They usually start out with things that are petty and close to home, but eventually they dig deeper and move further away from themselves. They start, say, with a sister stealing favorite outfits and end up listing world hunger. Once they have finished venting, this map, like the Enthusiasm Map, goes into the notebook for future reference.

Figure 2.3

Best/Worst List

This is another brainstorming activity, one that we keep in the front of our notebooks. It begins with the whole class creating a list of items that most of us might have a "best" and "worst" example of. For instance, we might have a best birthday and a worst birthday. A best restaurant and a worst restaurant. This list can offer many starting points for essays in multiple genres.

Best/Worst List Possibilities

birthday	class subject	car trip
restaurant	sport	meal
holiday	vacation	game
present	book	field trip
amusement park ride	movie	school project

Figure 2.4 A starter list for Best/Worst Possibilities

Figure 2.4 lists some category possibilities, but students will supply you with more. For any item on the list, students merely list their best and worst experiences, separated by a slash. For example:

Birthday: Disney World trip/cake eaten by dog

Restaurant: Olive Garden/diner in Hudson

Amusement park ride: the Tilt-a-Whirl/the Rotor (I puked)

Again, the idea is to get students thinking about their own lives, their own likes and dislikes, their own experiences and reactions to those experiences. Then, when they go to look for topics, they will have some on hand almost every time.

Spheres of Interest List

Another way of looking at potential topics is to ask students to think about their spheres of interest and influence. I ask them to imagine themselves at the center of concentric circles: immediately outside themselves are their own personal interests and everyday lives, beyond that circle is the local community and the school they attend. For many younger students, fifth or sixth graders, for instance, that is as far as their sphere of reference extends. Beyond the local community and school, there are state issues (like standardized testing), then national issues (like presidential elections and the issues that come with them), then world issues (climate change, terrorism), and finally universal/metaphysical issues (science topics like black holes and string theory, as well as religious or philosophical questions). As students get older, their spheres of interest should begin to extend outward, not just as writers, but as people. Writing can help students begin to extend those circles outward. I'll put the following list on the board, and ask students to add examples of issues that could be added as potential writing topics.

Spheres of interest: Issues that interest me, bug me . . .

Personal: cartoons, football . . .

Home: TV usage, chores, which way the toilet paper should face . . .

School: gum, homework . . .

Local: litter, nowhere to skateboard . . .

State: standardized tests, severe weather . . .

Country: Internet dangers for teens, presidential election, capital punishment . . .

World: climate change, terrorism, war, poverty . . .

Universe/metaphysical: religious issues, philosophical issues, science issues like string theory, cloning, black holes . . .

One thing we note when working on this list is that some issues can fall into more than one sphere and some (perhaps the best ones to write about) can be both national and personal. If the military and war are national issues, they are also personal issues if you have a sibling deployed overseas.

I will sometimes assign an essay to come from a specific "sphere" so that we can discuss how the "size" of the topic influences how you write about that topic. Writing about the school flip-flop policy requires a different kind of thinking than writing a paper about the war on terror.

Ongoing Topics List

As the year progresses, I ask students to begin looking for topics everywhere. At my household (where our children are unfortunate enough to have two English teachers for parents), if we find ourselves complaining about some injustice in society, some ludicrous behavior or attitude that we've observed, some moronic policy we see being enacted by local or national government, we will find ourselves saying, "Sounds like a 'My Word.'" We usually don't actually write a "My Word" due to lack of time, but we frequently find ourselves having opinions and wanting to express them. I try to encourage my students to do the same.

I ask students to set aside a page at the front of their notebooks (the fronts of their notebooks are very crowded) and keep an ongoing list of possible writing topics—this in addition to things that they may already have thought of on their various maps. It sometimes helps to remind them to add to this list on a regular basis, at the start of class every Monday or Friday, for example. Just make it a habit. My ideal is for students to have so many topics to choose from that they won't get to them all and can take some to high school with them. I also keep a list like this myself, and I sometimes share it with them.

Issues Bulletin Board

A class-wide strategy for keeping "big issues" in the forefront of students' minds is to create an issues bulletin board where you tack interesting articles, editorials, and printed Internet stories about various issues. It creates a centralized place for students to go and find provocative things to write about.

Personal Credo

This can be a writing assignment unto itself, or simply a brainstorming activity. A credo is a statement of belief, not necessarily in a religious sense, though it can be, but definitely in a philosophical sense. This assignment is good for students on a number of levels: it helps them clarify their values, it makes them put those values into words, and it gives them more ideas for things to write about.

To get students started, I simply have them write the words "I believe…" at the top of a piece of paper. I tell them they should rewrite those words on each line of the paper and follow it with a new statement each time. I tell them the statements can be deep or silly, sublime or ridiculous, general or specific—but they should be things they really believe.

I believe Ben and Jerry make the world's best ice cream.

I believe we should stop having wars and instead have international games of Ping-Pong to decide world conflicts.

I believe that we need to live creatively.

I usually set a time limit on this when it's an activity and tell students that the object is to keep writing no matter what—as long as it's all true. Again, this can become another source of topics for them to put into their overloaded notebooks. But it can also turn into an essay in its own right.

National Public Radio (NPR) has a feature every Monday morning called "This I Believe." Listeners write their own personal credos and read them on the air. The statements are all very different, very personal, and quite fascinating. The NPR Web site (http://www.npr.org/templates/story/story.php?storyId=4538138) has a complete print archive of all the "This I Believe" essays, as well as audio files of the authors reading their own essays. This is yet another example of real-life writing, and one that can produce some startlingly strong writing. Some of my students' essays moved me and opened my eyes to what they have been through, and what they hope for in the future.

Flash Nonfiction

In some ways, you are continually "setting the stage" for student writers. In my classroom I try to duplicate, as closely as possible, the conditions that real writers work under. But even grown-up writers spend time honing their craft, reading books about how to improve as writers, and even doing exercises from some of those books. I have read Julia Cameron's *The Artist's Way* and *The Right to Write*, both of which give specific journaling exercises, as well as writing books by Peter Elbow and William Zinsser that have suggestions for specific writing activities that are not polished pieces in and of themselves, but may help writers hone the skills they will use on those polished pieces later.

If there is one common thread throughout all of the arts, it is the idea of discipline and practice improving your skills as an artist. Musicians have finger exercises; singers do vocal warms-ups; visual artists have sketchbooks. As a cartoonist, I have a sketch pad where I jot down ideas for strips or series of strips as well as doodles. I assign myself little exercises: try drawing the same character's face with as many different expressions as possible, or try drawing a character doing some new action, or from a different angle. These sketches and initial ideas never make it into the newspaper like my finished comic strips, but they contribute to the quality of those finished strips.

When I teach middle schoolers writing, I try to think about it as I would an art class or a cartooning class—I want polished final works of art, but to get to those, I need to assign smaller sketches to develop various techniques involved in the bigger piece.

I have heard these exercises called many things: Show-me Sentences, Detail Paragraphs, Quick Writes, and just plain Journals. I tend to avoid calling them journals, simply because I think a journal is very personal—a free-form account and reflection on one's own life. These exercises are more focused and teacher-generated. I had thought of calling them "Writing Sketches," but that lacked something—probably alliteration. The name that seems to have stuck in my classroom is Flash Nonfiction. They are quick, focused writing assignments, for use either at the beginning of class or as homework.

Usually, I explain the Flash Nonfiction assignment and give students about five to ten minutes to complete it, depending on the length. When they finish, I ask them to pair up and share with each other. I usually give them something to focus on as they read each other's writing, which helps keep them on task. For example, I may ask them to pick out the best detail, find the most vivid verbs, or make one suggestion for a place that needs more detail. The sharing usually only takes about four minutes. Time permitting, I ask for volunteers to share either some whole exercises, or maybe just one good detail from their papers (which means that more people can share).

Assigning Flash Nonfiction as homework has its advantages as well. You can start class with the pair/share activity, but only students with the homework done get to participate. You can be done with the pair/share and group discussion in anywhere from six to ten minutes and then be on to the rest of the class.

A Different Kind of Practice

If you've been thinking these writing exercises sound like good ways to practice writing to a prompt for the state writing test, you are correct. But there's a difference here: some teachers teach using nothing but state test–style prompts, and all the teaching is geared toward test performance. The purpose of writing exercises I provide throughout this book is first and foremost to hone their real-world writing skills; the test is incidental. If you focus on writing exercises mainly as a way to better test scores rather than to better writers, you defeat both purposes, and neither test scores nor writers themselves are likely to improve.

CHAPTER 3

Content Dictates Form:
Ways to Organize an Essay

Most "traditional" elementary and middle school writing instruction about
organization amounts to the following: have an introduction, a supporting idea in
each of your three middle paragraphs, and a conclusion.

I have heard all the arguments in favor of this structure: it is all students can handle; it is a
good "crutch" for lower-level writers; it teaches them structure. I have even heard claims that it
teaches students to think.

Actually, teaching students how to think is precisely what it does not do. This formula
teaches students to avoid thinking except at a very minimal level. And teaching this structure
means teachers don't have to think much either. This structure isn't about thinking at all. It is
about filling in the blanks.

THE FORMAT OF THE FORMULA

Here is how the formula looks:

This is my essay about _____. My main idea about this topic is
_____. My three reasons for thinking this are 1_____,
2_____, and 3_____. Now I will tell you why.

First, _____

Second, _____

Third, _____

That was my essay about _____. My three reasons were 1_____,
2_____, and 3_____. I hope you agree with me.

I have seen templates not much different from this in many writing resources for teachers. On our state writing test here in Florida, essays that read almost exactly like the example above might earn passing scores, but then again, they might not. A score of 3 usually follows this structure and fails; a score of 4 follows this structure and passes. I will have to admit that when I look at the sample essays we receive from the state, many high-scoring essays are essentially more sophisticated variations on the five-paragraph formula. An essay scored as a 6 (the highest score) may still follow the five-paragraph structure, but with more details, more variety in transitions, and better word choices in general. But it's still the formula.

The Problem With the Formula

The argument persists (and I used to make it myself) that this structure teaches students the rudiments of organization, and that they can learn more sophisticated styles later. Well, *when* later? Because the longer students keep using the formula, the more ingrained it becomes. Many of them eventually resent doing anything different because to branch out beyond the formula requires extra mental effort. The Formula doesn't require that we think deeply about our topic or even care about it much. It requires that we fill in the blanks, get the job done as quickly as possible, and think as little as possible while we get it done.

Moving Away From the Formula

Thankfully, there has been a movement afoot for some time to move beyond the formula. In her piece "Toppling the Idol" (*English Journal*, 2004), Lesley Roessing shares how she moved from totally immersing her students in the five-paragraph essay to finally teaching them how to move outside the box. Her students "could write anything as a five-paragraph essay," which became "a template that every student's ideas had to fit into," but she moves away from the template, and in doing so, finds that she "now enjoy[s] reading their writings and so do they."

Abandoning the formula is not, however, just an opportunity for students to simply write free-form essays. To the contrary, abandoning the Formula means students will have to think, and think hard, about the structure of their writing, the flow of their ideas, and the total impact of their essays. This thinking will not occur as they draft, but before they ever start writing.

Real-world writers don't write in five paragraphs unless it happens "by accident"—that is to say, because after they had brainstormed all their possible ideas, then whittled them down and combined them, only three supporting ideas were left. They didn't set out to have five paragraphs—they just "happened" because that's what that essay called for. The content dictated the five paragraph form. Organization is about different ways of thinking about your topic, your audience, and the structure of your paper.

THE MANY WAYS TO ORGANIZE AN ESSAY

I teach my students that there are many ways to organize a paper, and if you look at a given topic, some organizational styles will work for that topic and some won't. What follows are descriptions of ways to organize a paper that I share with my students. I always tell them that this is *incomplete*. They will run into essays in their reading that combine two or more of these patterns, or, in the course of their writing, they may hit on an entirely new way to organize an essay that is not on my list. This is a starting point, though, and gets them thinking that there is a lot more to organization than simply throwing three ideas on a prewrite paper in no particular order and then starting to write.

Order of Importance or Stand-up Comedy Order

When in doubt, and they find themselves with reasons that won't connect any other way, I advise students to use Order of Importance. With this organization, they simply put their reasons in order from least strong (not weakest, one would hope) to strongest. But they don't stop there. They then take a trick from stand-up comedians. From what I've been told about stand-up comedians (I know only one personally), they tend to follow this pattern: start with your second-best joke, and then end with your best joke. In between those two jokes, you build from your least strong back up to your strongest material. Students typically grasp the logic behind this set-up immediately: start with a bang and end with an even bigger bang.

This, by the way, is another excellent argument against "making it up as you go." Most people, when improvising, will tend to begin their essays with their strongest, best reasons, and go downhill from there, ending with their weakest reason and ending their essay on a low note rather than a high one.

Chronological Order

This order is best for narratives—first one thing happens, then another, then another, and so on until the end. This is the organizational pattern students have been working with the longest, back to when they were writing "Once upon a time" at the beginning of their stories. But I tell students it can also be useful for other purposes. For instance, if they were doing an essay in favor of increasing or decreasing the amount of time allotted for class changes, they might wind up using Chronological Order to demonstrate how more or less time between classes would affect the campus. First, how would it affect the beginning of class-change time, when everyone is leaving class? Then, how might more or less time affect the class change time itself as far as hall traffic? Restroom time and locker use might also be given consideration. The start of the next class, after the longer or shorter break, could be considered. They are not really telling a story with this structure, but they are using Chronological Order.

Circular Chronological Order

This is a slightly more sophisticated style: instead of simply beginning at the beginning, you begin at the end. Many essays and pieces of fiction use this technique. They begin by talking about or hinting at how the story ends, then go back to the beginning. My favorite novel of all time, *To Kill a Mockingbird*, uses this technique by mentioning that the narrator's brother broke his arm when he was fourteen—an event that does not resurface again until the end of the story. This technique is frequently used in movies as well, where a narrative is "framed" as a flashback, and it can be used in narrative essays as well. In Robert Fulghum's untitled essay about an "unhinged" mother of the bride (from *It Was on Fire When I Lay Down on It*), the author begins by telling the reader that this is the "quintessential wedding tale—one of disaster." He doesn't tell what the disaster is—merely hints at it, then goes back to the beginning to tell how it all began.

Chronological With Insights

Again, a little more sophisticated than straight storytelling, this approach tells the story in chronological order, but it also stops the story itself to comment on it. Many of the "This I Believe" essays use this approach, as do many of the essays in *The Right Words at the Right Time*. An experience is related as it happened, and then analyzed—this is what the experience meant to me.

Spatial Order

If an essay involves describing changes in a specific place, for instance, a community, a school, or a household, then spatial order is useful. It goes from place to place within a locale, explaining or describing something about each place. For instance, if a student is writing about making a change on your school's campus, like adding security cameras, she could talk about how such a measure would affect different locations around the school. My earlier example of extending or shortening class changes could use this pattern as well: how would class change affect different areas of campus—the halls, the classes, the restrooms, the lockers?

Cause-and-Effect Order

This is one of the organizational patterns that requires the most forethought. The basic concept here is that if A happens, it will lead to B, which will lead to C, and so on. This pattern can be used for expository or persuasive purposes.

Let's look again at the idea of adding time to class changes. A student might say that adding one minute to class changes will make students more likely to stay in class once they arrive there. If they are in class more, there will be fewer distractions from "revolving door" traffic in and out of the room. If there are fewer distractions and more time spent in class for more students, then there will be more learning. If there is more learning taking place, this will enable students to someday compete in a global economy. . . . Okay, this can get out of hand, but it works up to a point. And it requires that students really look at the logic behind their ideas.

Affected People

This style of organization looks at the subject of an essay in light of the different groups of people it will affect. (Although when I list "affected" people, I picture someone putting on a fake British accent and putting on airs.) It is especially useful in persuasive writing. If you look at any controversial issue, it is controversial because it is going to affect various groups of people different ways. Let's say a student is writing persuasively about that old stand-by topic—gum chewing in school. If he wants to persuade the administration that gum chewing should be allowed, but gum "misuse" should not, he might look at how current and proposed gum-chewing policy affects different groups. The trick, of course, is to make it sound as if all the affected people will benefit from his side of the argument. If that isn't possible, a different organizational style might work better.

Compare/Contrast

This format is incredibly useful for expository, persuasive, and even narrative writing. It comes in at least three different varieties, and it is helpful for students to have all three varieties at their fingertips.

Comparison: Topic One, Topic Two

This organizational pattern is pretty self-explanatory. If you have two topics, you say everything there is to say about topic one and then everything there is to say about topic two. It's almost that simple. I do teach students, however, that there is a little more to it than that. Most of the time, both halves of the essay, both topics, follow a similar pattern. For instance, if I were comparing *Star Trek* to *Star Wars*, I might discuss the format, the fictional setting, the science-fiction trappings, the characters, and the themes and archetypes in *Star Trek* first. Then, when I discussed *Star Wars*, I would address the same issues.

This pattern also works for certain kinds of narratives comparing two events. Usually you will not want to mix up two different events but instead will narrate one and then the other. For instance, in Robert Fulghum's essay about musical chairs, he narrates first about his students playing the game traditionally (with people being eliminated) and their reactions to the game. The second half of the essay consists of a narrative of a more inclusive version of the game and student reactions to that version.

Comparison: Point by Point

This organizational pattern blends the two topics together, but does so, again, in a very orderly fashion. Each point of comparison is taken in turn, and both topics are examined side by side. For instance, the comparison between *Star Trek* and *Star Wars* might look like this as a prewrite:

Format
   Star Trek
   Star Wars
Fictional setting
   Star Trek
   Star Wars
Science-fiction trappings
   Star Trek
   Star Wars
And so on . . . .

Comparison: Similarities and Differences

Similarities and Differences is a variation on Point by Point—a more specific way of organizing the points themselves. It works when two topics have some very definite things in common that are important to point out, but also some equally important differences. All the similarities are grouped together, followed by all the differences, or vice versa. For instance, using the science fiction example again:

Star Trek *and* Star Wars *similarities*
   Faster than light-speed travel
   Space battles
   Many human-hospitable planets
   Alien races and humans interacting
   Epic themes of good and evil

Star Trek *and* Star Wars *differences*
   Setting and time period
   Types of battles/spaceships
   Forms of government
   Format (TV versus movies)
   Themes

Problem/Solution

This organizational style is simple, effective, and useful. The problem is vividly described, and then the solution is vividly described. The only danger I've found is that students will sometimes have such a good time complaining about the problem that they leave themselves very little time to make the solution vivid.

Geometrical Logic

The basis for this style of organization, used mainly for persuasion, is building an argument step by step. It is similar to Cause and Effect ("If A, then B"), but it isn't always the case that A happening causes B to happen. It is more like a proof in geometry (the only math class I ever truly loved): If A is true, then B will be true; if B is true then C will be true.

In my own editorial essay quoted in the introduction, for instance, I start with a factual premise: high writing scores on the Florida Comprehensive Assessment Test do not affect school grades; only minimum passing scores count. That's A. Given that premise, I then explain why the minimum passing score, which is not a great example of writing, becomes the score many schools "shoot" for. This shooting for a minimum score directly affects instruction and keeps "real" essay writing from being taught. I then explain how real progress in essay writing can be made, and how you can get great scores doing it. I conclude by saying that I will continue to value and teach excellence, even if the powers that be do not.

Be on the lookout for logical essays. They become harder and harder to find, unfortunately, as more and more public discourse, even essay writing, resorts to name calling and generalizations. But there *are* examples out there. One book I recently borrowed from a colleague, *The Pig Who Wants to Be Eaten: 100 Experiments for the Armchair Philosopher*, by Julian Baggini, is a series of philosophical scenarios that are argued to their logical conclusion. C. S. Lewis also writes very logically, but much of his work is both religious and difficult for middle school students. The essay collection *God in the Dock*, however, includes some more secular essays that are accessible for middle school students. They are excellent examples of logic. I have used "Meditation in a Toolshed," about the difference between objective and subjective thinking, with my eighth-grade classes for several years now to good effect. It is organized as a logical, comparison/contrast, main-idea-at-the-end essay—thus demonstrating how different organization patterns can be successfully combined.

End Reveal or Main-Idea-at-the-End

We often tell students that they must reveal their main idea in their introduction, and doing so is sometimes a good idea. But sometimes it's not. What if you could keep your audience in suspense for an entire essay? In the essay I just mentioned above, C. S. Lewis compares subjective thinking to objective thinking, asking us to consider which way of looking at things is more useful. He leads us through his line of reasoning but doesn't reveal his opinion till the very end. By doing so, he takes us on a journey with him so we see how he came to his conclusion.

If you've ever heard Paul Harvey's radio program, "The Rest of the Story," you've heard a master of this technique at work. Harvey gives his audience a series of facts about a person's early life, leading up to the moment when they finally found recognition, and then says, "And now you know the rest of the story." As you are listening, you are trying to see if you can figure out whom he is talking about.

Robert Fulghum used this technique in his essay about John Pierpont, a failed 19th-century social reformer, businessman, teacher, preacher, and lawyer. He lists everything that Pierpont failed at, only to reveal that each of us encounters a memorial to him each winter—a song he wrote called "Jingle Bells."

The Turn-About Essay

Sometimes the best way to argue your side of an issue is simply to knock down the opposing side's argument. "Turn-about" is fair play. It is possible to build an entire essay around an opposing side's objections. As a big animation fan, I have written several pieces about Disney animation. In 1995, when Disney's *Pocahontas* was released, I wrote an essay about people's objections to the movie. I built the essay around the objections, and knocked down those objections one by one. My arguments basically ran as follows.

> **Objection:** *Pocahontas* takes liberties with history—and that's bad.
>
> **My reply:** Then you'd better not let them watch Shakespeare's history plays, *The Miracle Worker*, or *The Sound of Music*.
>
> **Objection:** But this is aimed at kids—they're impressionable.
>
> **My reply:** Then discuss the movie with them. And remember that we give children simplified history all the time—remember George Washington and the cherry tree?
>
> **Objection:** But people will think Pocahontas really had hummingbird and raccoon sidekicks and sang Broadway-style ballads while she canoed.
>
> **My reply:** If they think that, they have intellectual problems a ten-hour Pocahontas docudrama couldn't cure. Consider a second possibility—the movie could spark interest in real history.

This essay was built almost entirely around people's objections to the movie. Only at the end do I give a benefit—sparking interest. Organizing your essay around the opposing side's arguments it often a very effective strategy.

PERSUASIVE-WRITING ISSUES

Persuasive writing is often considered the hardest kind of writing to do well, especially for student writers. In Florida, the state writing test scores are usually lower for the persuasive essay than for the expository. But testing aside, if our students are going to succeed at persuasive writing at more than a minimal level, there are certain issues we need to make them aware of.

There is no one way to organize a persuasive essay, but certain organizational patterns are very useful for a whole slew of persuasive situations. Here are a few suggestions.

Compare/Contrast

The big difference between a persuasive comparison and a typical expository comparison is that when you write persuasively, you need to favor one side of the two and pretty much put the other side down. This is especially useful for a topic that basically has two mutually exclusive sides. Remind students that it is very important that they clearly take a stand for one side or the other in the essay. I once had a writing textbook in my classroom that presented a straight comparison essay assignment as a persuasive assignment. I seldom used that textbook.

Cause and Effect

This format works well for an essay in which a change is being proposed. What immediate effects would be caused by the change, and what secondary effects might that lead to? In this kind of essay, a student could also describe one change, or cause, and numerous immediate effects, arranged by order of importance. If there is the space, cause and effect and compare-contrast can be combined. The student could show the causes and effects of leaving things the way they are, and then of making the changes he or she is proposing.

Other Important Persuasive Techniques

Too often we tell students to settle for elaborating some reasons, as if doing that alone will convince their readers to change their minds. There are other techniques that need to be considered when you write persuasively, and I try to make them aware of those issues in Flash Nonfiction exercises (see Chapter 2) and in drafts.

Framing the Issue: Why Is It Important?

Many times, before you can even begin to convince someone to take your side on an issue, you need to do a preliminary persuasive job—you need to convince them that the issue is worth looking at. There are many ways to frame an issue so that its importance will seem obvious. Many essays begin simply by talking about the many people who are affected by a particular issue. Sometimes a more personal approach is required, and the author tells a story readers can relate to in order to explain the importance of the issue. Sometimes just creating a word picture does the trick. *Orlando Sentinel* columnist Mike Thomas, writing about drivers with cell phones, began his essay by writing about Winnie the Pooh, SpongeBob, and other characters being gathered by a shrine along the curb. It turns out the shrine is dedicated to two young girls who were killed as their mother crossed the street with them in a stroller. The driver of the SUV that struck them had been talking on a cell phone. The issue is framed vividly.

Finding Common Ground

One of the things that distresses me as a teacher and as a citizen these days is the nature of our public discourse—we seem to be getting louder and shriller and more opinionated, and incapable of listening to anyone else's point of view. Many commentators and essayists seem to be preaching to the people who already agree with them rather than actually trying to persuade people to change their thinking. There are some columnists and essayists, however, who present a more thoughtful, and often more convincing, approach. One of the things these writers do is try to find some common ground with their readers. I often ask my students to do the same. What common principle, idea, or concept can people from both sides of an issue agree on? For instance, if we are debating gun control, both sides could probably agree that keeping guns out of the hands of criminals and the mentally unstable would be a good idea. Once we've established that, we can begin to talk about more all-encompassing gun control, or else very, very limited gun control, depending on which side of the argument we are on. If we simply launch into our side of the argument, knocking down the other side and calling them losers, we will not convince anyone.

Showing Your Understanding of the Opposing Side

Similarly, readers are more likely to listen to you if you show that you really know and understand both sides of the issue. If you come across as completely one-sided, never having listened to your opponents' point of view, you will have a hard time winning anyone to your cause. Take the ubiquitous old gum-chewing-in-school topic. If a student simply jumps in and starts calling the no-gum-rule stupid, very few adults will listen. If, however, a student begins by explaining how she understands the reasons for the gum ban, lists them, and says that they are understandable from a certain perspective, the adult, anti-gum audience is now listening. And now she can begin to make her points.

BEYOND THE FORMULA

When we simply ask students to reel off three reasons with as little thought as possible and then flesh them out with details, we miss the opportunity to teach them about the art of thinking. Part of that art is digging deeper into an issue to figure out what is really going on. The issue doesn't even need to be earth-shattering or affect the whole country in order to have even bigger issues at stake just under the surface. By moving beyond the five-paragraph essay formula, we give our students more opportunities to dig deeper—and become better writers.

CHAPTER 4

Prewriting: The Girders, the Skeleton, and the Frame

If we have given our students all these different patterns to use when they organize, when do they use them? Not while they are actually writing, except for mid-draft course corrections or for major revisions. Organization comes into play before you start writing.

The key to creating structured writing is thinking it out in advance. Narrative essays may flow naturally in chronological order, especially if you are relating events that happened to you, but expository and persuasive essays are trickier, their ideas become more abstract. If the ideas aren't ordered and structured, the whole essay may seem abstract and shapeless. Prewriting is the key to organization, because it gives you a way to map out what you are going to say, to see the "big picture" view of your essay, and eliminate, add, or change ideas around before you even start writing. It can really be a way of revising your essay before you even start writing it.

OVERCOMING PREWRITING RESISTANCE

For many years now, language arts teachers have been teaching students "the writing process," and as part of that process, we have taught "prewriting." In my experience, students usually hate prewriting. I have had many students refuse to do it over the years. For the most part, they refuse for two reasons. One, they think they write just fine by "making it up as they go." A prewrite kills their spontaneity and makes it less fun for them to write. The second reason, I think, has to do with the formula itself. If all you are doing is coming up with three main ideas, why bother with a prewrite? Who can't hold three ideas in his or her head? (Why should gum be allowed? Kids chew it anyway, it helps you think better, and enforcing the rule takes too much time.) If all you are doing is coming up with three quick ideas, using a prewrite seems like a formality.

But beneath these reasons lurks another reason: students are very seldom aware that real published essays are organized very differently, usually in a more complex process. They've never been asked to really analyze the way real essays are constructed—doing so is much harder than simply filling in the blanks of the formula, but also more rewarding.

I combat the "prewriting problem" (students avoiding prewriting) on several fronts: I ask them to read real essays, I try to show them the advantages of organizing in advance of writing, and I teach them that there are a lot of ways to organize an essay other than "list three ideas."

Analyze Real Essays

As I outlined in Chapter 1, when we read real essays, we analyze how they are organized. It is important to note that if you are using a lot of newspaper columns, as I am recommending, the paragraphs used are much shorter than paragraphs we typically want students to write. Some paragraphs are only a sentence or two long. I ask students to outline them, not according to the paragraphs, but according to the main ideas. Each main idea in a column may actually consist of several linked paragraphs. (This isn't a bad way to teach the reading concept of "main idea," either.)

Show How Prewriting Saves Time and Trouble

On a very practical level, prewriting makes writing an essay easier. I tell students that when you write, you are juggling so many things—specific details, sentences that flow, good word choices, addressing your audience appropriately—that if you can take organization out of the mix, it's one less thing to be juggling. If you prewrite, you never have to worry about what the next "big idea" in your essay will be—you can concentrate on fleshing out that basic structure. Many anti-prewriting students, when I press them, will admit that sometimes they simply run out of ideas halfway through an improvised essay. If you have an outline in place, you can save yourself a lot of trouble and even panic.

Demonstrate the Power of Outlining

An essay that is planned out tends to have more punch, more power, than an improvised one. I use numerous metaphors in class to make this point: the outline is the skeleton giving structure to the body; the outline is the steel frame of a building or car, giving structure to the whole building or giving the automobile the ability to move. I ask students to come up with their own metaphors, as well.

Prewriting Allows Playing Around With Ideas

When prewriting is more than just listing three ideas, it becomes a creative process. You can list many ideas, not just three, and then combine ideas that are redundant, eliminate weaker ideas, put ideas in a more logical order. You can play around with the structure of the whole essay very quickly to determine what looks as if it might work, and what needs to be changed. You can play around with how many paragraphs work best for your particular topic. You may need only four paragraphs to get the job done. Or you may need as many as eight. You might even need . . . five paragraphs! But if you use five paragraphs, you used them because the content of your essay demands it, not because an arbitrary formula does. This brings me to my number one adage for organization: content dictates form.

WAYS TO PREWRITE

I hope I have made a case that teaching the Formula is an easy way out that doesn't teach students much of anything. Teaching different styles of organization, on the other hand, teaches them not only how to write well-organized essays but also how to think logically and strategically as a writer. (I hesitate to use the term *critical thinking*, which has become so overused that it seems nearly meaningless to me.)

I have a tendency to distrust prewriting templates, because they often lead back to the Formula. Some of the templates I have seen actually look like the fill-in-the-blanks formula I presented at the beginning of Chapter 3. I prefer to have my students prewrite on their own paper. On the other hand, since there are so many ways to organize their ideas, it may be that some kind of formatting or template is useful in the short run. I offer a couple of templates here that students have found useful, and which I actually use myself.

The Two-Column Prewrite

This prewrite format is useful and quick, and gives students a chance to think about their ideas before they commit to using them. The basic format looks like Figure 4.1.

PREWRITE	
Topic/Main Idea	
A. Brainstorm	**B.** Organize Organization pattern: Ideas:

Figure 4.1

The area at the top of the T-chart is obviously for stating a main idea for the essay. Column A is for brainstorming ideas. I always emphasize that students are not to brainstorm three ideas and then stop. They are to brainstorm as many ideas as they can come up with. If they can only get three, fine, but three is not the goal. Ten is better for starters because it gives them more to work with. Once they have brainstormed, they mark up this A list. They should combine ideas that are too similar (e.g., my friend is fun, we have a good time together). They should circle or highlight their strongest ideas—the ones most likely to result in good, full paragraphs. We call these ideas "paragraph-worthy." They should also cross out ideas that are too vague or not strong enough ("not paragraph-worthy"). Once they have brainstormed, combined, and assessed for worthiness, they are ready for column B.

Column B is for putting the paragraph-worthy ideas into some coherent shape. Students should look at their ideas for an inherent pattern. Are many of their ideas places? Then they're probably looking at spatial order. Are many of their paragraph ideas about people? Then they're probably looking at affected people. And so on. If they are not hitting on any particular organizational style, they may decide to use my "default" pattern—order of importance. Once they have hit on a pattern, though, they should write down their main ideas in column B in the order that they will actually use them in the essay. This process doesn't actually take much longer than doing only a one-column prewrite. What it does do, though, is make students think about their ideas and how they fit together. It is the style I eventually recommend they use on their prewrite paper for the state test.

This process, like any process, must be modeled and taught. During Flash Nonfiction exercises, I have students write both columns on the overhead or board and explain their reasoning. We also critique their final outlines to see if we agree with the way they have ordered their ideas, whether the ideas hold up to scrutiny, and how the overall flow of the proposed paper works (see Figure 4.2). You can tell a lot about a paper that hasn't even been written yet by looking at the outline.

QUESTIONS FOR CRITIQUING AN OUTLINE
1. Do any of the ideas not fit the main idea of the essay?
2. Is each idea different—could any be combined?
3. Are any of the ideas too vague to produce good details?
4. Are there any ideas that the audience won't "buy" because they involve stereotypes, generalizations, or ideas that are easy to refute?
5. Should the order of the ideas be changed for better logic or overall flow?

Figure 4.2

Four-Square Persuasive Brainstorm

I reserve this prewriting strategy for longer, in-class, persuasive assignments. It is a way of making sure you have a fairly complete look at both sides of an issue or argument. Obviously, you divide a paper into four squares (see Figure 4.3).

SIDE A ARGUMENTS	SIDE B COUNTERARGUMENTS TO SIDE A
SIDE B ARGUMENTS	SIDE A COUNTERARGUMENTS TO SIDE B

Figure 4.3

I know this looks a little confusing. You need to talk students through it a couple of times, modeling it on the board. In the first column, Arguments, you simply argue each side of the issue: Side A and Side B. For instance, we used this format to debate a controversial bike trail through part of our community. Figure 4.4 shows how column A looked. Everyone in class had an opinion, and added ideas to support his or her opinion.

SIDE A ARGUMENTS—FOR THE BIKE TRAIL	SIDE B ARGUMENTS
The Trail . . . is safer than riding with traffic and is a particularly safe place for families and children to bike. creates a safe place for people to enjoy scenery without being in a car. promotes physical fitness. brings in eco-tourism dollars.	**The Trail . . .** will ruin a natural setting. will create traffic problems. will create litter problems. will bring in a criminal element. will encroach on residents' lawns. will invade residents' privacy.

Figure 4.4

We then gave each group a chance to create counterarguments to the opposing side, although a student can brainstorm these counterarguments on both sides on her own when she is prewriting alone. As a class, my students developed the following counterarguments.

SIDE A ARGUMENTS—FOR THE BIKE TRAIL	SIDE B COUNTERARGUMENTS TO SIDE A
The Trail . . . is safer than riding with traffic, and is a particularly safe place for families and children to bike.	The trail is not necessarily safer, as parts of it will still run very close to the road.
creates a safe place for people to enjoy scenery without being in a car.	The trail isn't necessarily safe, and some people bike and walk now without a trail.
promotes physical fitness.	You can be physically fit by going to the gym or biking on the road.
brings in eco-tourism dollars.	Eco tourism will bring lots of people we don't want into our front lawns—complete strangers who might be criminals

Figure 4.5

SIDE B ARGUMENTS	SIDE A COUNTERARGUMENTS TO SIDE B
The Trail . . .	
will ruin a natural setting.	The makers of the trail are not allowed to touch even a tree limb without permission.
will create traffic problems.	The trail helps avoid traffic problems by keeping bikers and walkers off the main street.
will create litter problems.	County employees check for litter once a week, but the population that uses trails is notoriously neat.
will bring in a criminal element and increase crime.	We'd have to research bike trails, but no one in the room had ever read about such an increase actually happening.
will encroach on residents' lawns.	Like a regular sidewalk, the bike trail would mean you'd have a little less to mow!
will invade residents' privacy.	How much "private" stuff do residents do on their front lawn?
will make it so some bikers use residents' front lawns as outdoor bathrooms.	There are bathrooms at both ends of the eight-mile portion of trail, which is only a half-hour ride. This argument doesn't hold water.

Figure 4.6

What do students do with this kind of brainstorm now that they're done? They need to shape it to fit their argument. They may need to create some counter-counterarguments at this point. Chances are they will organize it as a compare-contrast essay. This format for brainstorming gives students a more in-depth look at both sides of the issue, as well as a chance to gather a lot more potential support. The very process of doing this kind of "visible debate" sometimes changes people's minds—including the writer's. Some students who were against the trail began to decide that the reasons against it were not very strong and changed sides. This is part of the power of writing that we don't discuss much when we are teaching to the test: writing may not just change other people's minds—the act of writing sometimes changes *your* mind as you write.

GRABBERS AND CLINCHERS

One final area of the overall flow of a paper to consider is the way it begins and ends. In the Formula, we tell students to "Tell them" the main idea in the introduction and to "Tell them again" in the conclusion. If you read some real essays, you'll see they almost never tell you and then tell you again in exactly the same way. More often than not, published essayists imply their main idea at the beginning and make it explicit at the end, or else they state it at the beginning and give it an added twist at the end. Sometimes they don't let you know till the very end what they are talking about.

I'm not against a "thesis statement" and restatement at the end, but a strong essay certainly needs a lot more than that. In my class we call opening sentences "grabbers" and closing sentences or paragraphs "clinchers."

Introductions/Grabbers

Some people call these "leads." I prefer "grabbers" for middle schoolers, because it actually states what an opening should do. Like any list in this book, I consider this list of grabbers incomplete, and I always tell my students to look for new and interesting types of grabbers in our reading to add to the list or to invent new types of grabbers for their papers. The examples I use with my students for this subject actually do come from a state test topic: persuade a friend to stay in school and not drop out, for example. I don't use it because it's necessarily a fantastic topic, but because it lends itself to all of these kinds of grabbers. Most topics don't lend themselves to every kind of grabber. Again, content dictates form. Writers should choose the grabber that best fits their topic.

Asking the Reader a Question

If a writer wants immediate reader involvement, this is a good way to go. ("Are you thinking of dropping out?") A question gets readers thinking automatically—answering the question for themselves. The question should obviously have something to do with the topic at hand. The question can be asking the reader to relate to some universal experience ("Don't you hate it when…?"). A good question could be more open-ended as well. ("Is compulsory education for all students really a good thing?"). The audience may not quite know where the essay is going with the subject and not revealing the author's stance until all the evidence has been examined is a good way to create suspense (yes, suspense!) in an essay.

Starting With a Surprising Fact

To start with a surprising fact, you need to *know* a surprising fact—except, of course, on a state writing test, where students can make up facts and statistics on the spot and use them as long as they sound convincing. I'm not sure what the state thinks this practice is getting them ready for in the real world (a career in advertising or politics?), but I find it objectionable. (More on that later, in Chapter 11.) In any case, in real in-class essays, I tell students they have to back up any surprising facts. This may require less research than you might think. If your students are writing about topics that are important to them, they may already have a lot of useful information on hand. Basically, you find something a little shocking (or at least interesting), and start your essay with it. ("High school dropouts, on average, make thousands of dollars a year less than high school graduates, much less college graduates.")

Using Vivid Description (creating a picture)

The next chapter will have more about creating word pictures and teaching students to create them. For now, note that creating a picture—something specific—right from the start draws readers into an essay. The verbal snapshot might be of a person, place, or thing affected by the topic. Or it might create a compelling picture of a hypothetical situation. ("Picture yourself five years from now. You'll park your beat-up used car, don your little work visor, and spend the day saying, 'You want some fries with that?'")

Telling an Anecdote

Starting out with a very small story that illustrates what's at stake in the essay also brings readers in. People love stories. The story could be told in dialogue, narration, or a combination of both. ("You slammed your books on the desk, stood up, and stormed out of the classroom. I know that's the moment you decided to drop out.")

Using a Metaphor

Again, there will be more on metaphors in the next chapter, but for now understand that the right metaphor can not only start off your essay with a jolt, it can also hold the whole thing together. A metaphor can give us a picture of a topic that might otherwise remain vague and ethereal. ("A marathon runner is sprinting down the last mile of his 26-mile course. Suddenly, just as he nears the finish line, after all the effort he's put in, he stops, goes to the side, and sits down. He gives up, when victory was in his grasp. That's you.*)*

Having a Strong Thesis or Main Idea

This is my last resort—simply starting with your thesis. If nothing else will do, then go for it, I tell my students. But, if you're going to start out hitting us over the head with your main idea, do it with style. Don't just say, "Don't drop out of school!" To make a thesis into a grabber, you must toy with the catchy or maybe even tricky turn of phrase. Often, a catchy thesis statement will use a parallel structure or phrase to make us think. ("Dropping out of school is the worst idea you've ever had, and it will not only show your ignorance—it will increase it.*)* In this case, the contrast is between the two ways dropping out will interact with ignorance—it reveals it, but also makes it worse.

Conclusions and Clinchers

Clinchers and conclusions are often harder than grabbers and introductions. Most of the time when a writer uses his or her best material in the grabber, anything at the end of the essay feels redundant. I find that my students struggle with this section of a paper more than almost any other. Looking at real, published essays has led me to a conclusion, however, which is that most real essays go out with a brief, bright flame of ideas, rather than fading out for a long time. Clinchers should be short—sometimes as short as a sentence, or even a word. They certainly don't need to rehash all the ideas of the supporting paragraph as the Formula teaches us. With that in mind, here are some suggestions for ending essays.

Restating the Main Idea

I'll start with the main idea method since I just left it. Again, as with grabbers, it's the catchy turn of phrase with the parallel structure that does it. And that catchy turn of phrase can be very difficult to come up with. ("It isn't just a question of not dropping out of school; it's a question of staying in school and doing your best.")

Reviewing Cause and Effect

Rather than merely repeating ideas, it is good to step back and look at the big picture. What are the potential causes and effects involved in the issue? In the big picture, what will be the results, either negative or positive, if people accept the thesis of the essay? ("If you drop out, then you won't be able to have your license, but going places in a car will be the least of your worries—your life will be stalled out.")

Compare/Contrast the Two Points of View

Ending with a very brief, one- or two-sentence comparison of the two points of view in a comparison gives the ending a lot of punch and sums up the whole essay without necessarily being repetitious. ("Drop out, and you'll be closing yourself off from all kinds of possible futures; graduate, and you'll be opening doors to yourself to be able to do whatever you can dream of.")

The next few clinchers should look familiar because they also made good grabbers.

- Create a picture: *Here's where you'll be in five years if you drop out: living in a one-room apartment you can barely afford, driving some old scrap heap of a used car, and hanging out with . . . no one. Everyone else you know will have moved on in life, to college, to better jobs. You won't be moving at all, except backwards.*

- Ask a question: *Is that the kind of life you want to live?*

- Make a strong statement: *You won't be dropping out of school; you'll be dropping out of life!*

Circular Grabbers and Conclusions

Better than a great grabber and a great but disconnected clincher is a circular grabber-clincher that ties the whole essay together. A circular grabber-clincher shows forethought and planning. It takes readers on a journey and then brings them home again. It has form and symmetry. It's just good style. Best of all, it's pretty easy for student writers to do.

Use a Worst-Case Grabber and a Best-Case Clincher

This strategy begins the essay with a picture of the worst that could happen if the writer's suggestion is not taken, the idea not put into effect. Then, at the end of the essay, the writer gives the best case scenario—what could happen if the suggestion is taken. These scenarios will usually take the form of word pictures.

GRABBER: *Here's you, a year after you've dropped out. You're still living at home because you can't afford to get your own place, working at some job you hate, and your friends will all have moved on in their lives—without you.*

CLINCHER: *Here's you, a year after you've graduated high school. You'll be living in a dormitory on campus, taking classes toward a degree so you can get a job in a field you love, and most importantly, looking forward to your future.*

Extended Metaphor Grabber-Clincher

Let's say we've compared graduating high school to running a race, as we did above. Grabber: *A marathon runner is sprinting down the last mile of his 26-mile course. Suddenly, just as he nears the finish line, after all the effort he's put in, he stops, goes to the side and sits down. He gives up, when victory was in his grasp. That's you."*

In the clincher, the metaphor appears again. *Instead of quitting the marathon, the runner stands, tells himself the end is in sight and the goal is worth winning. He starts to run again, picking up speed, and then he finally goes all out and breaks the ribbon. All it took was a little more effort, and the prize was his. It's worth it. Are you going to finish the race?*

Question and Answer

If you start with a question, end with the answer.

GRABBER: *Are you thinking of dropping out of school?*

CLINCHER: *You can't really be thinking of dropping out—you're too smart for that.*

Anecdote/Story

If you begin a story in the Grabber, finish it in the Clincher.

GRABBER: *You slammed your books on the desk, stood up, and stormed out of the classroom. I know that's the moment you decided to drop out.*

CLINCHER: *Not long after you slammed your books down in class, you saw the rest of us at lunch talking about our plans for the future—for college, for the jobs we wanted. I saw you looking at us and thinking. You were starting to have second thoughts about dropping out. Listen to those thoughts.*

CLINCHER TO THE CLINCHERS

We owe our students more than "Think up three ideas and write them down." Organization is about a lot more than filling up three blank spots in a prefabricated prewrite. Organization is about playing with ideas, ordering ideas, using ideas well and logically, and putting ideas on display to their best advantage. But remember, the big ideas are only the framework of an essay. What we build on that framework is even more important, because it is what our audiences will actually read.

CHAPTER 5

Picture This!

Teaching writing is not just about getting students to have skills. It is really about honing student writers' instincts. Writing is not algebra, where you master certain skills and can then easily apply them to any similar problem. You may learn a skill in writing, and then proceed to write an entire essay without using that skill. Or you may not know how to apply an old skill to a new essay topic. Writers need to develop not only writing techniques but also an instinct for when and how to put those tools to use. One of our greatest challenges is to sharpen our students' instincts toward specificity. For whatever reason, most students tend toward vagueness.

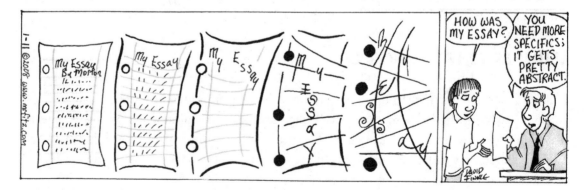

If the previous chapter's motto was "Content dictates form," this chapter has as its motto a quote from Stephen King's book *Writing: A Memoir of the Craft*: "Writing is mental telepathy." I have made this quote into a poster at the front of my classroom. Many writing manuals and textbooks talk about using specific details, but then either give no specific details themselves about how to "do" details, or they go into a lot of details about using adjectives. What good writers do, if you actually read examples of their writing, is to apply the old adage "Show, don't tell." But if students are to show and not tell, they need some specific advice on how to create those details.

GENERIC WRITING

Sometimes a nonexample will teach students the value of a writing skill. Nothing makes you long to have good proofreading like seeing a paper littered with mistakes, and nothing makes you want to be more specific than experiencing the mind-numbing effects of vague writing. One of my favorites to spring on my students is one that has appeared as a prompt on our state test in Florida: Explain why someone is a special friend.

This topic almost invariably results in a deluge of nearly identical essays. The names are different, but the details are anonymous and vague. My friend is fun. My friend is funny. My friend makes me laugh. My friend listens. My friend is there for me. My friend helps me with my problems. I really like my friend. My friend is the best friend anyone could ask for. My friend is awesome.

My essay is dull.

It almost never fails. I will read sentences aloud to the class and ask them to identify their own sentences when they hear them. They can't do it; all the sentences sound exactly the same. We give this type of prose a name: Generic Writing.

Generic writing seems to be the instinct of many, if not most, student writers. I am not sure why this is, but I know that calling students' attention to it is part of the solution. The other part of the solution is to develop new instincts. Some specific skills are involved, but they are all bent toward getting a writer to the point where it just feels weird to be vague. More on that later.

Modifiers and "Dead" Verbs

In surveying several of my district's adopted and unadopted writing texts (those free samples are still floating around my room), most of them have excellent sections on modifiers. In fact most of these texts give the impression that if you have enough sparkling adjectives and adverbs at your command, you can be a good writer. It seems to be the crux of the whole matter.

I couldn't disagree more. Adjectives and adverbs are the bane of most student writers: they lean on them like a crutch, and build entire essays around them. Stand-alone adjectives and adverbs are the main ingredients in many students' essays when they should merely be seasoning. Adjectives and adverbs create Generic Writing of the worst kind: essays about friends who are *fun, funny, awesome,* and *good.*

And what is the enabler of these rampaging modifiers? State of being, or what some of us are calling "dead" verbs: *is, was, were, are, be, has, had, have,* and so on. But teaching students to avoid dead verbs has perils of its own. I have had many students obediently circle all the dead verbs in a rough draft, and then obediently remove them—without replacing them with something better. I then wound up with entire papers made up of modifier-centered fragments.

So I address the idea of dead verbs and overreliance on modifiers, but I don't overstress them, because to do so is to focus on the negative; instead, I want them to focus more on what they *should* be doing: creating pictures.

Drawing With Words—Creating Pictures

After I've established the idea of generic writing with my students, I introduce the Stephen King quote, "Writing is mental telepathy." I have to explain what mental telepathy is. These days, students think it means talking on a cell phone. Once we've established that it's the rather science-fiction-y idea of sending your thoughts directly into another person's head, or receiving someone else's thoughts into your own head, we begin to apply the idea to writing. Why would Stephen King say such a thing?

At this juncture we return to their special, fun, funny, awesome, good friends. With these words, have we sent anything into our readers' heads that they can see? If all we've given them is adjectives, then they pretty much have to supply their own ideas. For writing to be mental telepathy, we need to give our readers something to latch onto—something to *picture.*

Dramatic Pictures

The following idea for a lesson is a little edgy, a little crazy. I have had more than one administrator come into my room to ask me if everything was "okay." But students always remember it, and, more importantly, they remember the point.

After we have talked about mental telepathy, I write a sentence on the board: *The teacher was angry.*

I then ask the class if I have used mental telepathy. Can they picture the teacher? Some say they can. I'll ask them if they are picturing some teacher they have had getting angry, and they'll admit they are. That, I tell them, means that they're supplying their own details. They aren't seeing the teacher I want them to see, because I haven't created a picture.

"But what if I said it like this?" I ask the class. I then act out the following sentence, bellowing at the top of my lungs, and actually performing each action: "The teacher slammed a book on the floor, tipped over his chair, threw an eraser across the room, and yelled, 'I'm not going to take this anymore!'"

At this juncture, anyone who was getting drowsy is now sitting upright, and the entire class is gasping in shock. This guy is nuts!

After they all calm down and the eraser, book, and chair have been returned to their rightful positions, we discuss the two sentences, which I now write on the board.

The teacher was angry.

This sentence has a subject (the teacher) with a dead verb (*was*) and an adjective (*angry*). This sentence, as we previously noted, contains no picture.

The teacher slammed a book on the floor, tipped over his chair, threw an eraser across the room, and yelled, "I'm not going to take this anymore!"

In this sentence we get the same subject (the teacher), but we also get strong verbs (*slammed, tipped, threw, yelled*) and concrete nouns, actual items we can picture in our heads (*book, chair, eraser*).

I tell them that this difference, between telling and showing, between generic writing and mental telepathy, is the key to nearly all good writing.

Once they understand the difference, the real work can begin: honing their instincts.

Writing Technique: Prewriting for Pictures

I discussed how the "writing process" can become a rote formality for many students, something they do to please the teacher rather than a meaningful activity that actually helps them write. I do think, though, that prewriting can be a useful tool for helping develop students' writing instincts, to make thinking habitual. A prewriting technique that I have found useful in helping students be more specific before they even begin drafting is a noun/verb T-chart.

Once students have outlined the main ideas for their paragraphs, I ask them to create a T-chart for each paragraph that looks like the one in Figure 5.1.

NOUNS	VERBS

Figure 5.1

I ask them to look at each idea and write down specific nouns that they associate with the paragraph topic. For instance, for "my friend is fun" they might list the following: water balloons, milkshakes, light-bulb jokes, tilt-o-whirls, homemade board games, tape-recorder radio shows. The idea is to list specific objects that an audience could see in their heads as they read.

I then ask them to list possible strong verbs that might "go" with each of those nouns, sometimes directly, sometimes not. The final list might look something like the one in Figure 5.2.

NOUNS	VERBS
water balloons	throw, pummel, splash, soak
milkshakes	slurp, freeze (brain freeze), spewed
light-bulb jokes	till, laugh, double-over, tear up
tilt-o-whirls	whirl, scream, lean, crush each other, spin, pull
trees	climb, hide, swing, hang
tape-recorder radio shows	record, announce, parody, sing, joke

Figure 5.2

I tell students this is a tool they can use to hone their "detail instincts." They can abandon it once their natural inclination is to create pictures when they write. Some students may not need to do it at all. But a chart like this doesn't take much time to create, and it virtually guarantees that every paragraph will be packed with specifics.

I model this process of brainstorming nouns and verbs with the class, take suggestions from them, and then model how to turn all those details into a paragraph. It makes them think about their subjects in new ways. I also tell students that the brainstorming process isn't always linear, with nouns first, then verbs. I may do a noun and verb, a verb and a noun, or else brainstorm all verbs first, and then add the nouns. It depends entirely on the topic.

Figure 5.3 is an example of a noun-verb chart for a narrative about bringing home a bad report card.

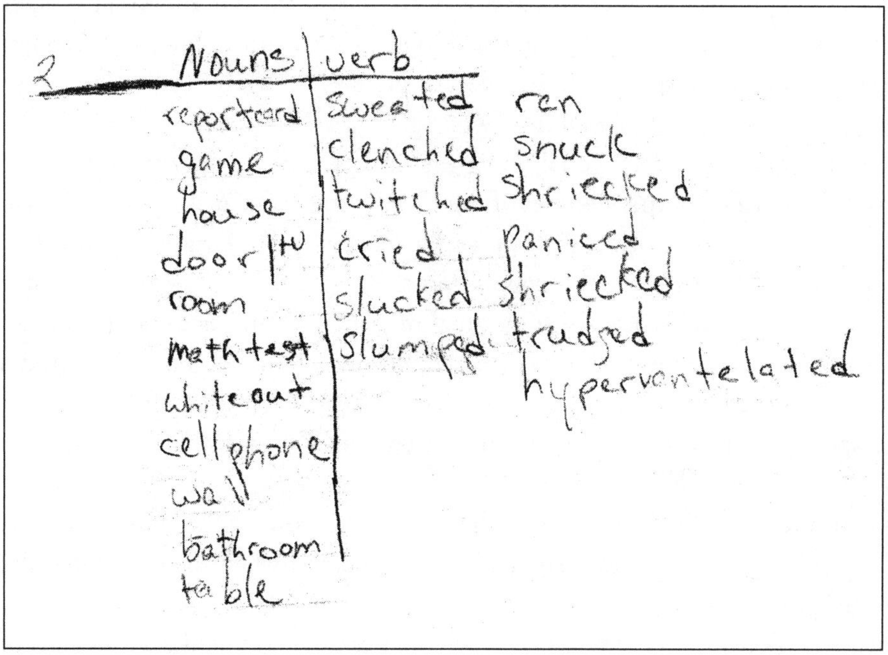

2	Nouns	verb	
	reportcard	sweated	ren
	game	clenched	snuck
	house	twitched	shriecked
	door/TV	cried	paniced
	room	slucked	shriecked
	math test	slumped	trudged
	whiteout		hyperventelated
	cellphone		
	wall		
	bathroom		
	table		

Figure 5.3

Writing Technique: Choosing Details

Some students may go overboard when they discover this technique of being specific. They may overload their essays with details, and those details may vary in quality or in their level of support to the main topic. A good exercise for the overly detailed student is this: think about the main point of your paragraph or essay, and go through your draft highlighting everything that is both a great detail and a perfect illustration of your main idea. If it isn't a great detail and/or doesn't really relate to your main idea, it should probably go. Some especially verbal students do need to learn how to "cut out the fat"—they simply write too much.

The Power of a Well-Placed List

We tell our students to use details, but avoid merely listing them. But on occasion, there is nothing like a good list. Most students have seen *The Sound of Music* on TV at some point and been exposed to the Rodgers and Hammerstein song "My Favorite Things." The point of the whole song is simply to list specific things you can picture. Sometimes a list of specifics from a prewrite may turn directly into a section of writing.

If you start looking for them, you'll find great "lists" in a variety of places. One of the best I've seen is in Robert Fulghum's "Mother of the Bride" essay from *It Was on Fire When I Lay Down on It.* The stressed-out bride starts to sample food in the reception hall before making her grand entrance for the wedding. Fulghum sets the stage for what is to come by not just telling us she ate lots of food, but by listing the things she is eating: she "sampled first the little pink and yellow and green mints. Then she picked through the silver bowls of mixed nuts and at the pecans. Followed by a cheeseball or two, some black olives, a handful of glazed almonds, a little sausage with a frilly toothpick stuck in it, a couple of shrimps blanketed in bacon, and a cracker piled with liver pâté."

Of course, the bride then throws up as she reaches the front of the church. But the list sets it up. You are there. You can see it. Lists can be overdone, but when the situation calls for one, there is nothing quite like one.

I sometimes ask students to see what part of their essay might lend itself to a list of specifics. If they look at their prewrites and have a long list of closely related items, they might want to use those items pretty much "as is" in their story.

Film Terminology and Details

A concept that has come into vogue recently is teaching "media literacy" or "film literacy." Students are taught about film lighting, film angles, and the various kinds of shots, and then they analyze film clips for these elements. Most of the resources I have seen that utilize this technique fail to make the obvious connection to writing, however, and there *is* an obvious connection. The different types of shots, from long shots to extreme close-ups, represent different levels of detail.

Watch, for instance, the opening credits of the first *Back to the Future* movie with your students. A long "pan" shot takes us across a close-up view of Doc Brown's laboratory. The details tell a story: a series of inventions are set in motion by an alarm clock going off, and we see an automated coffee-making, automated breakfast preparation, and automated dog feeding all going haywire. It shows us things about the character that lives there, and it also develops exposition (we know he's been gone for a while because of how things like the dog food are piling up).

Almost any movie will contain establishing shots that set the scene, and most of these will use long shots, medium shots, and close-ups to show us the setting and establish atmosphere. The close-ups are especially worth looking at: what details does the camera focus on, and what are they meant to show?

If we familiarize students with terms like close-up and help them think cinematically, if we can help them notice the close-ups in movies and find the "word close-ups" in the things they read, we can help them work on their own level of detail. It gives them a terminology they can relate to; most of them are familiar with movies, even if they aren't the most observant of viewers.

I've used a few different writing exercises based on movie terminology to help students use more detail.

One we call the Series of Close-ups, modeled on that opening scene from *Back to the Future*. I ask them to describe a room, but from a small-view, close-up perspective. Each sentence should address one small object or pair of objects, or one small place in the room. If we can move along the room spatially, from one place to the next in order, that's even better. To make it even more challenging, focus in even tighter: close-ups on only a person's desktop, dresser, kitchen counter, computer table, or locker . . . the list goes on.

Another variation is the Long Shot/Close-up. Describe a scene—a classroom, a school yard, a mall, a living room, a movie theater—as a long shot first: big impressions, overall view. Pretend the camera is moving in, and focus in a little tighter: one section of the scene, one group of people or objects. Then focus on a couple of people or objects, then on one. Finally, describe the one person or object in great detail.

The reverse of this exercise is also useful: focus on one object or person, then draw outward till you reach the larger scene that gives context to the original object.

These may sound like fictional techniques, but they have implications in other kinds of writing: all problems that affect the big picture also affect the individual (long shot to close-up). What affects the individual also affects the big picture of society (close-up to long shot).

Challenge students to pick a problem (teen suicide, depression, dress codes, censorship) and present it in cinematic fashion. It makes for a good grabber or clincher to an essay. In their prewrites they might even draw a series of pictures, a storyboard, of details they wish to include. Another technique might be to write three columns on the prewrite paper—long shot, medium shot, close-up—and then to create supporting "picture" details under each column. The idea, as always, is to get them thinking visually.

When we discuss "movie-style" details, it is also a good time to talk about what to leave out of the frames you create for your pictures. Just because a detail is specific doesn't mean it supports your cause. If you're complaining that the food in the cafeteria is disgusting, then mentioning that you really, really like their chocolate chip cookies they serve doesn't support your main idea. There is such a thing as "too much information."

Figurative Language

There are other forms of detail at a writer's disposal besides concrete details. One of them is figurative language. The problem is that metaphors and similes are difficult to use, especially if you want to use them well. An e-mail I have received several times over the last decade lists the "Worst High School Metaphors," supposedly from student papers.

The little boat glided across the water exactly the way a bowling ball wouldn't.

John and Mary had never met. They were like two hummingbirds who had also never met.

Here is what I've found: many students have trouble thinking of metaphors or similes at all, and many of them can produce them, but aren't very good at it, so you almost find yourself wishing they hadn't even tried.

The solution here, as always, is to find and observe good examples of metaphors in "real" essay writers' works. When and how do they use them? What makes them work?

Metaphors can be serious or amusing. Students should be aware of the effect they are reaching for. Dave Barry, for instance, is the master of the bizarre metaphor. In his essay about his fear of scary books and movies, "Confessions of a Weenie," he piles metaphor upon metaphor. He invents a fictional monster called the Brainsucker, then metaphorically divides his brain into two sectors: the SAT Sector (all logic) and the Fear Lobe (all fear). He then has the Fear Lobe telling him that his backyard "is exactly the kind of place that would attract the

Brainsucker. For the Brainsucker, this is Walt Disney World." Soon, even the SAT Sector is scared and "has soaked its mental armpits." That last phrase just floors me. A sector of his brain has "mental armpits" to soak.

Ask them to listen for metaphors on TV shows or look for them in comic strips. On the sitcom *Seinfeld*, Elaine's dancing is described as "a full-body dry-heave."

On a more serious note, metaphors can be used to make a concept crystal clear—especially in persuasive writing. We tend to think of persuasive writing as very left-brained, serious business: "Just the facts, ma'am," as they used to say on *Dragnet*. Yet persuasion, if it is to be effective, must engage the whole brain of the writer and the reader. If we are going by "just the facts" to persuade our audience, we are likely to be dull, and when we are dull, we are unconvincing. A metaphor shakes up our thinking as readers, makes us see the topic from a new angle, in a different and unexpected light—and may make us agree with the essay writer.

I often ask my students to bring newspaper columns into class as part of our Adopt-a-Columnist project (see Chapter 1). I ask them to take special note of how often, and how, their writers use metaphorical language.

One syndicated columnist, Kathleen Parker, uses metaphors in nearly every essay. In today's newspaper, she writes about artists who try to enrage religious leaders with sacrilegious images. Near the end of column, she says, "Those who taunt true believers, meanwhile, are like children trying to get a rise out of daddy. A mature father knows to ignore the brats."

This neatly skewers both sides of the debate: the easily offended religious leaders become, by implication, immature fathers; the artists who taunt them become, in essence, brats. Whether one agrees with this assertion or not, the image it evokes of the dynamic involved is hard to refute: we all know that some people are just looking for a reaction, and that others should know better than to give one.

Pull out any newspaper and read the columns—not the official newspaper editorial, which tends to be drier and more generic. Almost any column you pull up will include metaphorical language to give you a different way to think about the subject at hand. Here is a sampling of metaphors, pulled with almost no effort from recent newspapers. I am not explaining the circumstances that gave rise to these metaphors, merely noting their use.

From the first sentence of a column by George Diaz: "I like to think of George Crossley as a modern-day Don Quixote."

Sometimes even the title of a column is metaphorical, and the writer builds the entire essay around it. Robyn Blumner titles a column about overworked employees, "Denying Overtime Akin to Slavery."

Even some of the most logical writers of all, scientists, are forced to use metaphorical language to express their most complex ideas to a general audience. Thus Carl Sagan in his book *Cosmos* compares the history of the universe to a calendar in which the Big Bang occurs in the first seconds of January 1st, and the entire history of the human race takes place during the last few seconds before midnight on December 31st. Here the metaphor is not only clearer than the numerical facts, but it also has the power to make us gasp.

In his essay "A New Theory of the Universe" in *American Scholar*, Robert Lanza tries to explain that time, from a physicist's perspective, is an illusion, by comparing time to a record album: "depending on where the needle is placed, you hear a certain piece of music. This is what we call the present."

Metaphors are not just for poets. If we want our students to use decent metaphors, we must point out examples of them—and they are everywhere—and discuss their use and misuse.

In addition to finding examples of metaphor in print all around them, I try to get students thinking metaphorically more often, about things large and small. What is the mess in their backpack like—an archeological dig? What are people with ear phones and headsets like—cyborgs?

Extended Metaphor

In addition to using metaphors within an essay, students can be taught to use extended metaphors to run through and structure an entire essay.

This technique goes far beyond the usual formula-writing "My three reasons are…," yet it is in the grasp of most middle-school writers. Again, looking at essays from published writers, it is fairly easy to find examples. In C.S. Lewis's essay "Meditation in a Toolshed," he examines the differences between objective and subjective thinking by using the metaphor of a sunbeam shining through a hole in a toolshed. Looking at the beam from the outside, you get one experience; looking along the beam to see what is outside the shed gives you another experience. Lewis goes on to give multiple examples of looking *at* and looking *along* things (examples that create pictures, I might add). But in the end he comes back to the sunbeam in the toolshed, coming to the conclusion that you must look at *and* along things to know them fully, and that looking only at them is not just unwise, it is virtually impossible.

Brainstorming Metaphors

Getting students to think metaphorically doesn't need to wait until students are drafting—they can think ahead and do it while they are prewriting. In addition to listing concrete nouns and strong verbs, I often ask them to brainstorm lists of possible metaphors to use. What is a metaphor for the main point you are trying to make? What metaphors would demonstrate your supporting ideas? Students need practice with metaphorical thinking, and giving them small writing topics that require them to think metaphorically—such as in the examples below, is a good way to provide that practice:

How is school like a business? Who are the customers? Who are the employees? What metaphors, positive or negative, could describe MySpace? If you view MySpace as positive, is it a web of connections drawing people closer together, a virtual studio for self expression, a tool for connecting people—sort of the modern equivalent of talking into Dixie cups attached by strings? If you view it as negative, is it like a spider's web luring people into trouble, a spreading virus, a cyber slingshot to hurt people long-distance?

Hyperbole

Another technique that published writers frequently use and that we underutilize (or at least relegate to the occasional poetry unit) with our students is hyperbole. This is a shame, because hyperbole is more fun than all the theme parks in Orlando combined.

Again, look through published essays to find examples. One essay I share with my students is "Neat People Versus Sloppy People" by Suzanne Britt (see Appendix C). Her unusual thesis, that "Neat people are lazier and meaner than sloppy people" always intrigues students.

She compares neat people to sloppy people, and the neat people come out wanting. She uses a host of specific details about things that sloppy people save, but her barbs for the neat are mostly hyperbolic. A neat person, she says, "will sell a La-Z-Boy recliner while you are reclining in it" just to keep the house neat.

Again, start searching for examples, and they'll jump out at you. Hyperbole can be used for comic effect, as when Dave Barry insists that the hotel rooms at Disney World are "clean enough for neurosurgery."

Hyperbole is usually a better tool for expository and personal essays than for persuasion. Most of the time it's too, well, overblown for persuasive writing.

This technique can be difficult to use effectively, yet students love it once they get the hang of it. How do you get student writers to "get the hang of it"? Again, exposure to good examples and practice. It's important to point out examples of hyperbole to students as they appear in essays; students often read right over them without noticing them for what they are. As far as practice, I again think prewriting may be the perfect place to brainstorm possible uses for hyperbole. Which ideas lend themselves not just to details, but to exaggerated details?

Hypothetical Scenarios

Another writer's tool I have never seen explicitly taught but observed often in published essay writing is the hypothetical scenario.

Especially in persuasive writing, where we are asking our readers to consider alternatives, following the differing possibilities to their logical end gives us a contrast that will, if handled properly, make our side of the argument sound favorable.

Columnist David Broder, writing on the Democratic and Republican strife about how to end the war in Iraq, proposes what each party should do. "Democrats," he says, "should concede one big point: Absent any readiness on their part to cut off funds to the troops in Iraq, those forces will be there as long as George Bush wants them to remain." He then changes gears and says that Bush "should be called upon to pay attention to the Democrats' demands— and the public opinion that supports them."

Broder is creating a "here's what should happen" scenario. This may not actually cause the scenario to come to pass, but the scenario itself may influence people's thinking about a given situation.

An *Orlando Sentinel* My Word essay by a local rabbi argued against an ordinance that would prohibit feeding the homeless in a local park. He proposed a "public, peaceful gathering outside City Hall, led by the religious leadership of Orlando to dissuade our city from enforcing city ordinances that seek to forbid feeding the homeless . . . ." Sometimes a scenario is more than hypothetical . . . it is a potential scenario, and an author is calling on members of his audience to take action.

To get students thinking hypothetically, especially for persuasive essays, I ask them to list the two opposing sides of a given issue. If each side had its way, what would it look like? Give us a picture. Give us a hypothetical person for each side. Give us a hypothetical school, city, country, or world. What would the opposing sides look like?

DETAILS AND AUDIENCE

One other issue that I bring up with my students is that the details they choose will vary with their intended audience. One of the ways I sometimes annoy myself, though, is by talking to my students about audience issues when I know full well their writing is never actually going to have an audience (other than me). There will be more on solving that problem in the final chapter. The other problem I have is that much of the essay writing we are likely to read or write, especially in this day and age, is for a general readership. Who is the audience for an editorial? For a blog?

Too Informal

I tell students, "Don't turn off your audience—because if they don't like your tone or your attitude, they may simply stop reading." Students need to be very careful not to insult their audience. If they are using precise details—strong verbs and concrete nouns—they are probably avoiding the kinds of vague adjectives that will be insulting: *stupid, dumb, rotten,* and so on. A lot of the time, though, it is the adjectives students will sometimes pin to their details that change their tone as writers. There is a big difference between saying you wish the cafeteria French fries could be hot and crisp, and saying the cafeteria French fries are limp, greasy, and ice-cold. The first is more diplomatic, makes the point, and may not insult the cafeteria workers. The second is going to put adults on the defensive. The challenge is to avoid being insulting, yet not tone down the writing till it's bland.

Too Much Formality

When students write for a private audience of their peers on their phones or online, anything goes. When they write for their peers, but an adult audience may be reading, too (say in the school newspaper), they have a delicate balancing act. When they write for an adult audience, they sometimes err on the side of formality so that all the life is sucked out of the writing along with the word *sucks*. They may resort to adjectives and impressive thesaurus words. The challenge is to find the right details for the right audience.

PROMOTING PICTURE MAKING

There are many ways to create pictures, and many ways to teach students to create them. There are other ways to reinforce the ideas that good writing is all about the pictures, before and during the writing process.

Flash Nonfiction

Keeping in mind the model of an artist's studio, I'll return to the idea of Flash Nonfiction, where I write a topic sentence on the board, something that might be a paragraph within a larger essay, but certainly not a big enough topic to fill up an entire essay (at least not for most students).

I then give students about ten minutes to write off the top of their heads on the topic, encouraging them to use as many specific details as possible. We then spend some time pairing up and sharing the results. I go around and listen as they share. To give them focus, I'll ask them to pick their partner's best, most vivid detail and highlight or circle it. After this pairs activity (which takes only a couple of minutes), if there is time I will sometimes have two or three volunteers read their entire paragraphs aloud to the class. Again we will compliment and comment on the best details, the things that created pictures. This is a simple but powerful exercise because they write and get immediate feedback.

If you can't spare that much time, then Flash Nonfiction makes good homework: it's quick and easy to do independently. The sharing part can then be your class opener the next day, and students look forward to it.

What kind of topics do I give? Almost anything that lends itself to a short paragraph. Any topic can be taken and given a particular twist. Give students a specific audience—the type of details you use will change. Some of them, I'll admit, are generic state-test types of topics.

But while these are not necessarily going to produce great essays, they are perfectly suitable for quick exercises. Other topics are more like topic sentences—they fill in the details.

1. Explain why you think one thing about your school stinks.

2. Persuade the principal to allow or not allow cell phones in school.

3. Explain why you think students drop out of school.

4. Explain why a particular television show is your favorite.

5. The roller coaster was scary.

6. It was an interesting classroom.

7. She was a total snob.

8. Persuade a friend to not drop out: use an extended metaphor.

9. The service at the restaurant was terrible/fantastic.

10. He/She was a terrible student.

11. He/She was an excellent student.

12. It was pitch black in the nighttime forest.

13. I made a mad dash to get to class on time.

14. I was nervous/happy as I brought home my worst/best report card ever.

15. My favorite game is...

This kind of short writing exercise can also be targeted to any particular skill you'd like them to practice sketching: figurative language, hyperbole, hypothetical situations, and so on. Simply give them a topic and match it to a writing technique. How would persuading your parents to give you a higher allowance look as a word picture? As a metaphor for something else? As a hypothetical situation? As hyperbole? You can recycle topics, giving them a different technique to use each time.

Again, I think of these as "sketches" like those in an art class. We are honing skills. The danger comes if the sketches become the end and not the means. Sketching should always be followed by a larger, more complex work that uses the skills you have learned by sketching; writing exercises should always be followed by a larger, more complex piece of writing.

The Picture This! School-wide Writing Contest

One other way to make writing part of your school culture is to create a school-wide, weekly writing contest. At our school we call it "Picture This!"

It runs on the same basic writing-as-sketching principle as Flash Nonfiction, and we use it to promote creating specific details.

Here's how it works. Most schools have an in-house TV news program at some point during the day, or at least announcements. The contest is featured each Monday on our news. The first week, I introduce a "showing" sentence and tell the student body that the contest is to create one, only one, sentence that shows us the same idea by creating a word picture. I created an entry box out of a shoe box and entry forms on strips of paper (see Figure 5.4).

PICTURE THIS! ENTRY FORM

This week's topic sentence:

My "word picture" sentence that shows rather than tells!

Please put your name, grade, and Language Arts teacher's name on the back of this form before entering.

Figure 5.4

I then collect entries in the box, which has the sentence posted on it, for the next week. We've tried having the box in the cafeteria and the media center, and have found the latter works better. The current list of sentences looks like this:

1. The room was messy.
2. The car was a piece of junk.
3. The hallway was crowded.
4. The storm was scary.
5. My friend makes me laugh.
6. The sunrise was beautiful.
7. I had a bad cold.
8. I laughed really hard.
9. The old house looked creepy.
10. It was a bad meal.
11. It was a good book.
12. The Buffalo wings were really hot.
13. I was really sleepy.
14. The roller coaster was scary.
15. The cotton candy was messy.
16. The backpack was overloaded.
17. The kitchen was filthy.
18. It was really hard.
19. We had fun.
20. The first day of school was really hectic.
21. The teacher was boring.
22. The cafeteria was a mess.
23. The substitute was angry.
24. His sneakers were very old.
25. It was a gloomy day.

Choosing winners is fairly easy: you eliminate the sentences that are fragmentary, vague, or incoherent. One entry from our very first contest about "The room was messy" read: "Roaches ridin' stink bugs!" You may be a little discouraged by the entries at first, but it is interesting that the longer the contest goes on, the better the entries get.

After weeding out the obvious nonwinners, you will have some possible winners left. Usually another teacher and I rank the finalists and come up with between two and five winners. We read the winners on the air, so the whole school gets to hear a few good examples of "mental telepathy" each week. The next sentence is announced, and the whole process starts again.

It is a very small investment of time for a pretty good payoff: it gets students thinking about creating word pictures school-wide, and it makes the task fun.

Another added activity, if you have an art club (or, as I do, a cartooning club), is to have other students make posters of the "Picture This" winning sentences. I would simply format the page with the original "telling" sentence at the top and the winning "showing" sentence at the bottom. A student artist draws a picture of the "word" picture in the middle. These posters bring it home that a good word picture is easy for someone else to visualize. We display these posters around the school, further reinforcing the idea that creating pictures is what good writers do.

It was a cold night.

"I curled up, still chilly, under a sheet, two blankets, a comforter, three pillows, another blanket, some of my sister's stuffed animals, and a purring cat."
Christopher Finkle

PICTURE THIS! WINNER
Topic sentence: The hallway was crowded.

Word picture: The kids were moving an inch an hour while the teachers were trying to direct where they go; only the little shrimps managed to squeeze their way through the bigger kids. – Mitch Lane

Topic Sentence: My friend made me laugh.

My friend jumped up on the table at lunch and started to do a mix between the chicken dance and the heel-toe, and everyone laughed so hard they shot jell-o out their noses. – Ian Manning

Prewriting Revisited

Most of my students come to me hating prewriting, as I noted in the chapter on organization, because it seems like extra work, and they think their essays are good the way they are. Prewriting can be used not only to organize ideas but also to brainstorm details. Students' writing skills are on a broad continuum, from students who almost never write a specific detail to students (usually avid readers) who use details often and well. At the less-specific end of that spectrum, it may be helpful to ask students to do more than simply write an outline. We may ask them to also make a list of all the details and types of details they can possibly think of. The purpose is neither to make all students brainstorm details on their prewrites (some of them don't need to), nor to expect students to brainstorm details forever. Eventually, they may no longer need to prewrite details in order to write with them. But in the interest of getting them to think more specifically, to develop their instincts for creating pictures, I sometimes ask students to use a prewriting form something like this.

ESSAY PREWRITE	
OUTLINE Brainstorm	Order
Word Pictures	
Nouns	**Verbs**
Movie details: Your topic as . . . Long shot Medium shot Close-up Extreme Close-up	**Well-placed list:** What ideas could appear as a list of specific details?
Figurative Language My main idea is like: My supporting ideas are like:	**Hypothetical Situations** If I had my way . . . If my opposition has their way . . .
Hyperbole Exaggerated details . . .	

ESSAY PREWRITE

OUTLINE Brainstorm <u>Save the ocean</u> global warming recycle / conservation	1) word picture Order 2) pollution, harm/danger 3) what you can do to help.

Word Pictures

Sunsets, dunes, sand, waves, the shore, animals

Nouns marine life - dolphins - turtles sunsets - birds horizon line - crabs white water - fish - reefs	**Verbs** destroying beautiful - killing - glistening as - choking the light bounces - polluted off the white cap - space ripples

Movie details: Your topic as . . . Long shot earth covered in water polluted air Medium shot sunset / waves on the shore Surfer → pipeline wave Close-up litter & marine life Extreme Close-up	**Well-placed list:** What ideas could appear as a list of specific details? - the sun shining on everything - 1/2 of US. population lives in a coastal zone - 1/3 of U.S. Gross National product is produced in a coastal area - 10 things you can do to help - put a famous quote about the ocean in between every paragraph

Figurative Language My main idea is like: The ocean is a very important component to all life. My supporting ideas are like: We need water and animals to continue the food chain. We would loose many jobs.	**Hypothetical Situations** If I had my way . . . no condos, no tourists, no litter, no cars on the beach If my opposition has their way . . . animals will die, water will become polluted, shore/ dunes will disappear, you
Hyperbole Exaggerated details . . . The entire world would be lost (barely exaggerated)	won't be able to see the sun on the beach because of the condos. Global warming!!

Highlighters

One way to make students see, and see vividly, how much of their writing is specific, is to give them highlighters and let them mark up their own or each other's drafts. The simplest form of this concept is probably best: highlight any part of this draft that creates a picture or uses figurative language or hyperbole. Whether they are marking their own or each other's papers, the feedback is immediate and concrete. The more of the paper that's highlighted, the better off the writer is, generally. The more white space, the more nondetails they have filled their papers with.

You may play around with multiple colors: green is for specific details, yellow is for figurative language, and so on. This gives them a chance to see how much of each technique they are using.

MAKING PICTURES THE HABIT

This chapter may seem heavy on exercises, but I again bring up the idea of creating a writer's studio: we sketch to hone our skills, and then we put our skills to work on a larger canvas. But the idea isn't just to drill discrete writing "skills," but to create new writing habits, and a "feel" for what works in writing. I certainly wouldn't go through every writing exercise listed here and then let students write longer essays only after they've "mastered" those skills. You never "master" writing skills—you have to learn to reapply them to every new writing situation. One of my eighth graders last year told me that when she took the writing test last February, she heard my voice echoing through her head: "It's all about the pictures, the pictures, the pictures!" And she did very well on the test.

CHAPTER 6

Avoiding Clunkers and Creating Sentence Effects

Once students are organized and beginning to create word pictures, a deadly disease of the student writing world can still kill their papers. Many students may have great details buried in muddled, incoherent sentences—what I call "clunkers." Clunkers are sentences that stop the flow of a paper. They may be unclear, wordy, or awkwardly patched together, and they are often nearly impossible to understand.

Many students aren't even aware that they are creating these little monsters, so they can't begin to eradicate them. But if you have ever sat and read 150 to 200 student essays, you know that this is where many, if not most, student writers fall down. Students write lots of awkward sentences, and they need simple, jargon-free strategies for trying to spot them and fix them. Take for example these gems:

Choices were made by some people that were bad because they caused the people to get punishments that were bad.

If you don't do these things, then your decor ends out in not matching and looks yucky, and not stylish, you don't want that.

This way of doing things causes some people to break out and brain go dark in what they to do.

If you've been teaching middle school language arts for any length of time (say, two weeks), you won't have to imagine a paper that consists entirely of clunkers like these. For a very large portion of students, creating sentences that make sense is a real problem. When I look at a student essay made up almost entirely of clunkers, my heart sinks. How can I help them? Well, as with so many problems, the first step is to get students to admit they *have* a problem.

RECOGNIZING THE PROBLEM

If you are going to teach students how to spot and correct clunkers, you need real, not textbook, examples to use with the class. When I deliberately try to make up a clunker, it simply doesn't work. A clunker almost always has a certain bizarre, organic antilogic all its own that can't be duplicated by merely adding mistakes to a correctly constructed sentence.

So, where do I find examples to share with students? From students, of course.

The Clunker File

I keep a running file of student clunkers from year to year on my computer. I collect them as I read over or grade papers (it only takes a minute to type them). If I want to use them immediately, I either change the details, keeping the faulty structure the same, or I leave the sentence "as is" but don't use it in the author's class. I may also get them from the Picture This! contest box I described in Chapter 4. Many of the entries are put out of the running not for their lack of detail, but for their clunkiness.

I use this collection both to create awareness of the problem and to discuss how to avoid and/or fix the problem. My first principle in pointing out flaws in anybody's writing is to make it clear that everyone makes mistakes. I show students my rough-draft clunkers so they can see that they can happen to anybody. Students become aware that they are a common ailment of rough drafts, not a complete anomaly, and that they are fixable.

Many student writers have the impression that good writers get things right on the first try, and that tinkering, revising, and making corrections are for losers. I try to show them the reverse is true. Good writers are good precisely because they do tinker and revise. Good writers seldom if ever get everything just right on the first shot.

I use my clunker collection in a couple of ways to create awareness. The simplest is to project actual examples in their original form and ask students to discuss what is wrong with them. We identify what makes the sentence not work. I don't give students a list of "things that make sentences clunky," either. I ask them to try to articulate what trips them up when they attempt to make meaning out of it. It may be slow going at first. Just as when they write, students often start out vague and need to be pushed to be more specific. "I just don't like it," and "It doesn't sound right," are typical early on in the process. But eventually I can get them to nail down what's wrong—without having to use any fancy grammatical terms: "There are too many words that don't matter." "We don't know who the word 'they' is talking about." "There are too many 'ands' strung together."

Another way of using clunker samples is to "fix" the sentence, and then have students compare the two versions. For instance, I might take the clunker, *They probably have enough money with all their wealth and riches to feed the world two full and healthy meals.* I rewrite it to read, *With their extra wealth, they could probably help solve the world hunger problem.*

I display both of these options and we discuss which one is better and why, again pushing toward specifics. Part of what we discuss is that sometimes it is not just the sentence that is clunky, but the thought itself. What exactly does that first part of the sentence mean? "They" have enough money to feed the world? The whole world, or just the impoverished parts? What does "two full and healthy meals" mean? Two meals a day forever? Two meals as a one-shot deal? From the perspective of clarity, it needs a lot of work.

Figuring out what is wrong with these sentences is not the same as fixing them. That's where it becomes difficult—but doable.

Fixing Clunkers Without Jargon

Once you've gotten students to recognize they have a problem, you may want to rush in to fix the problem by throwing a lot of grammar terminology at them. "You need to try using some participles! You need to use some gerunds! Add some prepositional phrases!"

Sadly, what we often do is confuse our students and turn them off even to attempting to solve the problem when we muddle things up with a lot of unnecessary technical terms.

Unnecessary is the key word. There are some terms our students will need to know. In their book *Getting It Right*, Michael W. Smith and Jeffrey Wilhelm give two "justifications for teaching a term:

1. The term is so commonly used that teachers, texts, and tests presume that students know it.

2. The term is essential to being able to explain an important issue of style or correctness." (Smith and Wilhelm, 2007)

Which terms are "common" and "essential" will vary from state to state, school to school, and even classroom to classroom. We'll talk more about how these terms may come into play later. For now, we'll bypass them and instead discuss some principles students can use to fix their clunky sentences.

The basic questions I tell my students to ask, and which I actually ask myself when I'm revising my own writing, are these:

- Is it clean?

- Is it clear?

- Do the parts connect?

Is It Clean?

Are there extra, "fatty," unnecessary words in the sentence which could be cut? This is one of the chief causes of awkward sentences. Take this real student example, for instance: *Second of all the next reason or characteristic a true and good friend should have in my opinion is generosity or being caring.*

Many students think that we want them to simply write more. Longer papers get better grades, right? So just throw a bunch of words in, make it as wordy as possible, and the teachers will eat it up! Everything in the sentence above is stated at least two ways: *second of all/the next*; *reason/characteristic*; *true/good*; *generosity/being caring*. The only thing stated just once is the superfluous *in my opinion*. We need to teach students to "cut the fat."

I use a variety of ways to get students to do this. Sometimes I ask them to start all over and state their idea in as few words as possible. Sometimes I will ask them to take their existing sentence, circle the main noun and verb, and then cross out every other word that isn't absolutely necessary. And if they're worried about the length of their essay, I tell them to add details, not fat!

Key question for writers to ask themselves: Which words aren't really necessary?

Is It Clear?

Does it make sense, or is the meaning buried somewhere in poorly ordered words?

Drawing harshly on there rough paper and then a swamp of ink kisses the surface then a napkin goes to smudge the ink and wipe out the picture before anyone welcoming it to the world.

I am exhausted by the time I finish a sentence like this, much less a whole paper full of this sort of rambling. This sentence may have a good idea buried somewhere deep inside it, but it is so hard to slog through that it's hard to figure out what that idea might be. In dealing with clarity issues, a number of technical terms may end up coming into play, chief among them parallelism. The nice thing about parallelism is that most students are aware of the concept from math class, so it isn't completely new to them.

I tend toward parallelism problems in my own rough drafts and have to be on the lookout for them. Our students need to be on the lookout for them, too. In sentences with parallel structures, all the elements have to "match up" or appear parallel to each other grammatically. This sentence has several things going on: someone is drawing on rough paper, the ink is kissing the surface of the paper, the napkin is smudging out the drawing. However, each event is written in its own verb tense, creating the disconcerting effect that they came from different grammatical universes.

Parallelism is one of the most common errors students make, but it doesn't even make it in to some middle school grammar books.

Key question for writers to ask themselves: What is making this sentence confusing, and how can I fix it?

Do the Parts Connect?

For longer sentences especially, connecting all the parts correctly is the major issue. Is it a run-on or comma splice, or do all the parts fit together the correct way? Take for instance this example: *All of a sudden you feel as if nothing bad matters and bad things will happen, but so will great things, and then you'll end up loving life to the fullest until another bad thing happens, then the process starts all over again.* This isn't exactly wrong per se, but the connections between the individual ideas aren't very good. The very first two items, *nothing matters and bad things will happen*, don't seem to fit together quite right. Then you have another section starting with *but* and two sections starting with *then* and *and then*. The whole thing goes on too long without really making a clear statement (see "Is it clear?" above).

As you deal with sentences like these, you may deal with the limited terminology I mentioned earlier: mostly terms like *run-on, fragment, comma splice, subject, predicate, noun, verb.* However, you might be tempted to venture further into the jungles of jargon by bringing up phrases, clauses, and words like *dependent* and *independent.* This may be necessary, but only if the terms are pertinent to the discussion of how to fix the sentence at hand. Gauge what your students can handle, and be aware that there are ways to talk about connecting sentence parts that don't involve a whole lot of terminology. More on the actual "fixing-up" process shortly.

Key question for writers to ask themselves: Do the ideas in my sentence flow from one to the other or do they get jammed up?

So two principles emerge for getting rid of clunkers:

1. Cut extra words that don't mean anything.

2. Make sure the words that remain DO mean something.

The three questions (Clean? Clear? Connect?) attempt to address those two issues. They are jargon-free, easy to remember, and easy to use. Next we'll consider *how* to put them to use.

FIXING THE PROBLEM

I said earlier that one use of my "clunker collection" is to create awareness of the problem. The second use is even more important. I use the collection to model how to improve clunkers and then give students practice in making improvements themselves.

Clunker Clinic

When I am introducing students to the idea of clunkers, we are simply noting what makes them "not work." Once we've all seen what the problem is, we work on trying to cure it. The name "Clunker Clinic" occurred to me one day, and it has stuck.

How It Works

The basic premise of Clunker Clinic is simple: I project examples of clunkers, and students rework them either individually or in small groups. We then discuss student solutions as a class. When we start doing the clinic, I model how I would fix a sentence, using the three questions (Clean? Clear? Connected?).

For instance, I might project this sentence: *Not even just the gross stuff is what I mean by being vegetarians are healthier though.*

I talk students through my thinking on how to fix the sentence. "Well, first I need to figure out what the sentence means. The writer is writing in favor of vegetarianism, so the 'gross stuff' probably refers to things that are gross about the way meat is processed, or about the act of meat-eating itself. So they are saying it isn't just the fact that meat is gross that causes vegetarians to be healthier—a vegetarian diet is healthier because of what they do eat, not just because of what they don't.

"Okay—I think I've got the meaning, but that meaning isn't clear here. I need to clean this sentence up. What words look like they're 'fatty'? Well, *not even just* could probably be cut down to size, as well as *I mean*. I'll circle those words for possible deletion. Now, what about 'Is it clear?' I think I've figured out the meaning, so I need to make that meaning shine through. Also, the first part of the sentence and the last are bridged by the words *is what I mean by being.* That doesn't seem to connect the two parts very well.

"So I could write, *It isn't just the fact that eating meat is gross that makes vegetarians healthier, though.* That works. It's clean—I can't see what else I would cut. It's clear now, I'm pretty sure. There aren't a lot of parts to connect because I cleaned up the connection that didn't 'work' when I simplified it."

Notice that in fixing up the sentence, I didn't use a lot of grammar jargon. Also note that I had to focus on the meaning, not just the structure. Clunkers are bad because they interfere with your reader's understanding what you have to say. The focus needs to be on meaning, not on terms.

WHOLE-CLASS CLINIC

After I model two or three sentences this way, I let the class try to help me out by offering suggestions for how to fix the sentence. We eventually settle on one that works. I will sometimes let the class give a "thumbs up" vote for a suggestion, and if that suggestion doesn't work for most of the class, we try another one. The idea here is that you are modeling the process involved in eliminating clunkers often enough that students can eventually internalize it.

SMALL-GROUP CLINIC

The next step is to put students in small groups, give them clunkers, and ask them to rewrite them. This may be the most valuable activity of all, because everyone needs to be involved, not just the few people who tend to raise their hands in class. The first time you do it, students may struggle to come up with good ways to fix the sentences, but with time they generally become more comfortable. I usually give each group the same clunker to fix, and each writes its new, improved sentence on large strips of craft paper to post at the front of the room. Each group then presents its version. We sometimes vote on which version of the refurbished sentence works the best—and why.

INDIVIDUAL CLINIC

Once we have practiced in large and small groups a bit, I use the clinic as a "bell-ringer," or start-of-class activity. I project a single clunker example, and students get five minutes or so to try to fix it up. I then have them pair up to discuss their solutions with each other, sometimes asking them to come to a consensus as to which version works best, and why. That "why" is very important. I then ask several people to share their solutions with the whole class. I will sometimes quickly type in their solutions onto my computer and project them as they read them aloud. It is fascinating to see how one awkward sentence can generate so many possible solutions. Here are some examples of students' solutions:

Original clunker: *Decisions were made by some students that were bad because they caused students to get grades that were bad.*

Student Rewrites:

- Some students' decisions were bad, causing them to get lower grades.
- Bad kids made decisions to disrupt the class, therefore the other students didn't do well.
- Some bad decisions made by students could cause lower grades.
- Some students made bad decisions, thus causing their grades to reflect those choices.
- Students made bad decisions, which caused them to make bad grades.
- Some students made bad decisions which reflected in bad grades.
- Some students' grades were lower because of their bad decisions.
- Some students made poor decisions, which caused them to get bad grades.

After listing some of the many versions of the sentence on the projector, we discuss them. The following is a transcript of a class discussion about the sentences above.

MR. FINKLE:	Which version of this do you think is the best? Obviously not the top one, since that was the original. Brendan?
BRENDAN:	"Some bad decisions made by students could cause lower grades."
MR. FINKLE:	Why is that one the best?
BRENDAN:	It just doesn't seem as clunky as the other ones. It just seems to work.
MR. FINKLE:	Is it clean?
BRENDAN:	Yes.
MR. FINKLE:	Is it clear?
BRENDAN:	Yes.
MR. FINKLE:	So it has all those things going for it . . . maybe. I'm not so sure how clear it is, myself. Does anyone have a different vote?
CLAIRE:	"Some students' decisions were bad, causing them to get lower grades."
MR. FINKLE:	Well—here's an issue with this sentence. What's wrong with "Some students' decisions were bad"? Do you know what that's called?
CLAIRE:	Oh, it's passive.
MR. FINKLE:	How could you state that actively?
CLAIRE:	"Some students made bad decisions…"
MR. FINKLE:	… which caused them to get lower grades.
BRENDAN:	The one I liked has passive voice, too.
MR. FINKLE:	Oh, yeah! You're right.
SHAI:	But I still think that one is the best—Brendan's.
JAKETTA:	Me, too.
MR. FINKLE:	What about this one? "Some students made bad decisions, thus causing their grades to reflect those choices."
SHAI:	It's too long!
BRENDAN:	It sounds like Mr. _____. (He mentions another teacher's name.)
MR. FINKLE:	What words aren't necessary?
SHAI:	"Thus."
MR. FINKLE:	Why?
SHAI:	It makes it sound too fancy.
BRENDAN:	It sounds like the Bible or something.

Ultimately, we decided that the final choice was the best of the imperfect choices. *Some students made poor decisions, which caused them to get bad grades.* This, they concluded, was the most active, simplest version.

We talked about the terms *active* and *passive* voice, because they had a direct impact on the decisions we made. We did not talk about clauses or phrases, because they simply didn't come into the discussion.

This kind of messing around and decision making about sentences is what writers do all the time. Discussions like these make the process visible rather than mysterious.

Finding Clunkers in Their Own Writing

Once they've practiced spotting clunkers with the class, students actually get quite good at it. The next step is to get them finding clunkers in their own rough drafts. The pain of finding clunkers in their own writing will have been lessened by the fact that they've seen that such bloopers are a common phenomenon, not just a product of poor writers. There are a variety of ways to get writers in the habit of rereading for clunkers.

Whoever is checking the rough draft for awkward sentences needs to have a way to mark them. If you have access to highlighters, they work well. I ask students to highlight clunkers in pink or orange—something that will stand out. If you can't get your hands on highlighters, underlining works (circling whole sentences gets sloppy and unclear).

Self-Check

The easiest way to spot clunkers in your own paper is to do it yourself, but many students will do almost anything to avoid looking at their writing after the rough draft is finished. When I am first teaching them to look for clunkers, I give them a specific time, sometimes a whole class period, just to look for and correct clunkers. They need to know it's a priority. When students are looking for clunkers, I offer them several suggestions for ways to go about it.

Read the whole paper straight through to see how everything flows together, marking clunkers as they jump out at you. Watch out, though. It is very easy to "fix" your own writing in your head as you write—if you are missing a word or two, or have words out of order, your brain will often compensate by reading what you meant rather than what you actually wrote. After all, you wrote it, so you know what you meant.

To avoid the problem of "brain fixes" when reading your own paper, read your paper backwards, sentence by sentence. Instead of focusing on the overall meaning and flow of the paper, focus on the meaning and flow of each individual sentence. Seen in isolation like this, sentences often reveal their hidden clunkiness.

Peer Check

Peer checks use essentially the same process—except that you are asking students to exchange papers. It is much easier to spot clunkers in someone else's papers—and more fun! Again, it is important to create an atmosphere ahead of time where students are aware that everyone makes this kind of mistake. Once papers have been exchanged, I'll tell them they are only looking for clunkers—no worrying about spelling mistakes or other kinds of errors, and no attempts to correct them. Simply highlight sentences that don't "work." I will usually ask the peer reader to use a different color than the author used. Again, reading straight through, then backwards, can be helpful. For many students, by the time they and a peer have looked their essay over, there may be very few unidentified clunkers left—but there may be some.

Teacher Check

When is the best time for a teacher to look over a paper for clunkers? I'm going to suggest that waiting for the final draft isn't the best idea. By then, students consider the paper a done deal that they don't need to change, and your comments or suggestions may very well be ignored. If you want your input to make a difference, the best time to check for awkward sentences is sometime during the writing process.

Check During Drafting

I know that one view of the writing process is that drafting is a kind of "anything goes" stage to get things down in some kind of form so it can be changed later. In this model, the draft is often called the "sloppy copy"; drafting and revision are two airtight, compartmentalized activities; and asking students to think about sentences as they write is tantamount to stifling their creativity. I disagree with this model—it doesn't match up with the messier process I go through when I write. When I am drafting with pen and paper, something I seldom do any more, I find that my drafts are sloppy not because of my hasty scribble but because of the number of times I cross out and rework sentences as I write. I revise as I go when I am on my computer "word processing," too, but since I immediately delete the older versions of my sentences, all evidence of it ever having happened disappears. This process is taking place now, as I write this paragraph, this sentence, even. I am revising while I draft this chapter.

So I talk to my students about revising sentences as they draft—especially for students who know they are prone to clunkers (as I sometimes am). I then circulate as they draft, specifically looking for clunkers they can correct.

I have discovered that drafting time, when students are writing quietly, is one of my best times to get some brief one-on-one time with my students. I circulate, and quietly ask if I can take a quick read-through of their essays. Sometimes I will skim through an entire essay, find no major mistakes, and try to give some positive feedback. Sometimes I will reach a clunker within the first paragraph. I stop and ask the student to read me the sentence aloud. Usually, attempting to read the sentence aloud will immediately call attention to the fact that there's a problem. Try reading aloud *Second of all the next reason or characteristic a true and good friend should have in my opinion is generosity or being caring*. It just doesn't sound right.

Once we've admitted there's a problem—the first step—we then talk about ways to fix it. I ask the student to rewrite the sentence more clearly, and I offer feedback on the quality of the revision. Within two to five minutes, we will have caught and solved one awkward sentence problem, and I will ask the student to try to continue that process as she drafts. This puts the responsibility back on the student. It's her paper, her clunkers, and her solutions—the problem is to be worked on, not ignored. Since drafting a single essay takes anywhere from two to four 45-minute periods in my class, I can usually get to everyone this way over the course of the drafting.

Check After Drafting

I don't often do this, but if I was so busy with other concerns (calls over the intercoms, fire drills, etc.) to do individual clunker conferences as students drafted, I will sometimes take up drafts and try to mark clunkers myself. I will usually do this after students have already had a chance to self-check and peer-check for them. Then I just skim through them with a third color of highlighter, looking only for clunkers. It's important that I'm totally focused on that one thing—if I get bogged down in other aspects of the writing, it will take too long, and I want to get feedback to them within a day. Once I hand the papers back, I ask them to look over the sentences I highlighted and see if they have any questions. They start to revise their papers (more on that in Chapter 9) and I start to take questions individually. Another new tool I have at my disposal is my own "wiki" Web site where I can view student drafts and make online comments for students to read. For more about wikis and how to use them, see the last chapter of this book, about publishing.

Check During Final Corrections

If you look over papers one last time before students write their final drafts, as I do, this will be your last chance to find the clunkers. Unfortunately, you will also be looking for spelling mistakes, punctuation errors, and a whole host of content concerns. It can be done, but it makes your job easier if the clunkers have already, for the most part, been dealt with. If I am looking for awkwardness at this stage, I simply put the big, traditional *AWK* in the margin and leave it at that, but there is usually much less time for dealing with those problem sentences this late in the game.

Sentence Effects

So, what kind of sentences *do* we want students to have? I once again ask my students to go into the works of published essay writers, into their columnists, to observe what those writers do.

At the level of the individual sentence, good writers try to state things as clearly as possible—unless they are, say, William Faulkner. Good writers avoid the kinds of clunkiness we've just finished fixing. But they do other more positive things as well that relate to the overall effect of their essay: they use a variety of sentence formats, a variety of sentence lengths, and sometimes they use fragments occasionally if it suits their purposes. One of the dirty little secrets of published writing is at last being talked about: Real writers use sentence fragments for effect!

Lengths of Sentences

In addition to getting students to be aware that there are different ways to construct a sentence, I also try to make them aware that different sentences create different effects in an essay. I ask them to look for those effects when they read essays; I ask them to work at creating similar effects when they write and revise.

Short Sentences

When I say "short sentences," I mean sentences that consist of short, complete, uncomplicated thoughts. They are most often simple sentences in the technical sense. Students are often afraid to write these sentences—they seem too "elementary school." But when used wisely, and not overused, very short sentences have tremendous punch. Short sentences can be used to create several sentence effects.

EMPHASIS

A short sentence in the midst of longer sentences stands out. If you make a short sentence its own paragraph, it especially stands out. In Robert Fulghum's essay about the mother of the bride, Fulghum has a description of the parents, groomsmen, bridesmaids, flower girl, and ring bearer entering the church. This description is full of medium-to-long sentences and ends with the bride entering, looking white, both from nerves and from the all the food she'd been nibbling in the reception hall. Fulghum describes her as a *grenade with the pin pulled out*. He follows up all of these longer sentences with a short, four-word sentence, sitting all by itself as a paragraph, *The bride threw up*.

The comic timing of that sentence, coming after the string of longer sentences, never fails to make students laugh and go "Ew!" at the same time.

Well-placed short sentences make you sit up and take notice.

CHOPPINESS

Choppiness is generally viewed as a negative quality in a piece of writing. But there are times it works in a writer's favor. This kind of choppiness is especially valuable in narratives—look at an exciting scene near the end of a novel and you'll find it used quite a lot. It creates tension. It creates suspense. Every sentence matters. You read more intently.

Choppiness can be used for comic effect as well. In Jerry Seinfeld's book *Seinlanguage*, he is discussing the power of television by admitting that he actually bought a Ginsu knife: *I can't believe I wrote the number down. I can't believe I called it.*

I can't believe I gave them my credit card number.

It's important that this be choppy—not a fluent, complex sentence. He isn't collectively disbelieving this event. He can't believe each step that he took.

In Bob Morris's essay "Needing the Fair," he describes the fair in short, terse sentences: *It has bluster. It has guts. It teases. It taunts.* So do short sentences!

SLOWER PACE

Oddly, although they are easy to read, short sentences sometimes slow the pace of a piece of writing. Having a period at the end of each thought is somehow like repeatedly hitting the brakes while driving a car. It slows things down, sets off each sentence in sharper relief. In his Mother of the Bride essay, Robert Fulghum describes the MOTB's satisfaction with the monster wedding she's created in two short sentences. *She had done it. She glowed, beamed, smiled, and sighed.*

In Dave Barry's "Confessions of a Weenie," he discusses his aversion to horror books and movies. He has one longer sentence, *I should know better than to read horror books, or watch horror movies, because—this is not easy for a 42-year-old male to admit—I believe them.* The next sentence is what slows us down, though. You can almost hear him saying it, slowly, and nodding: *I have always believed them.* Short sentences sometimes make us not only slow down but also imagine we can hear the author speaking.

Long Sentences

Longer sentences are in many ways harder to do well, but they create certain very specific effects of their own. I always emphasize that a long sentence does not happen by accident, just because you forgot to put periods. Long sentences are deliberately constructed, and there are certain effects you are attempting to create by using them.

FASTER PACE

Again, this may be counterintuitive, since longer sentences are sometimes harder to read, but I think longer sentences actually speed a text along. There are no breaks in the form of periods in a longer sentence. They speed along without stopping. They are good for describing complex ideas or actions that need to be combined into one idea or action. In Robert Fulghum's MOTB essay, he writes that after the bride has thrown up, *Groomsmen rushed about heroically, mini-princess flower-girls squalled, bridesmaids sobbed, and people with weak stomachs headed for the exits.*

In another Fulghum essay, he describes the end of the game of musical chairs: *And by jerking the chair out from under his opponent, one guy slams down into the last chair—a look of triumph on his face—hands raised high with forefingers signaling NUMBER ONE, NUMBER ONE.*

The faster pace helps create the sense of action.

SUSPENSE, EMOTION

Longer sentences can be used to create suspense and tension, especially in narratives. Dave Barry, discussing a horror novel character named Marge writes, *But Marge, in the hallowed horror-novel-character tradition, barges straight ahead, down gloomy corridors where she has to cut the foreboding with a machete, despite the obvious fact that something hideous is about to happen, probably involving the forced evacuation of her skull cavity by a demonic being with the underworld Roto-rooter franchise.*

A longer sentence can also create emotion, the sense that so much is going on at this point in the essay that it must all go together in a rush of words. Robert Fulghum, in his essay about John Pierpont, reveals that Pierpont, despite failing at every career he'd ever tried, was not a failure, because he wrote the song "Jingle Bells." His long sentence reads: *To write a song that stands for the simplest of joys, to write a song that three or four hundred million people around the world know—a song about something they've never done but can imagine—a song that every one of us, large and small, can hoot out the moment the chord is struck on the piano and the chord is struck in our spirit—well, that's not failure.*

Fragments for Effect

I was not introduced to the idea of fragments for effect until college, and when I was, I was immediately thrilled. I knew that fragments were bad from what my teachers had taught me. I also knew that "real" writers used them all the time (some more than others). I do think middle school students can handle fragments—under certain conditions. I make it an option for students who have proved they can generally write using complete sentences, and I make them identify their fragments for effect with a little *FFE* notation in the margin of whatever copy I will be proofreading, to let me know they put the fragment there on purpose. Fragments can be used like short sentences, for emphasis—especially emphasis for comic effect. They can also be used to create a more conversational tone when that's appropriate. Robert Fulghum is the king of the fragment for effect, and he uses it to create a very easygoing, conversational tone.

Take a look at these examples from the mother of the bride essay, in which the fragments for effect are italicized.

- I don't mean [the motb] was unhappy, as is often the case. *To the contrary.* She was overcome with joy.

- … this lady had been waiting with a script for a production that would have met with Cecil B. DeMille's approval. *A royal wedding, fit for a princess bride.*

- *Ah, the bride.* She had been dressed for hours, if not days. No adrenaline was left in her body.

When you try making those fragments part of the sentences, or complete sentences, they just don't work quite as well. A fragment duplicates the way people sometimes pause for emphasis and effect when they are speaking.

READING FOR SENTENCE EFFECTS

It is one thing to introduce students to different types of sentences in the form of notes or a reference sheet. It is another to get them thinking about sentences in their reading and using different types of sentences in their own writing. As your students look at published essays, asking them to look at how writers use sentence effects gets them to be more observant readers. It can also make them think about their own writing in new ways. There are a variety of ways for students to analyze how writers work.

Analyze the Effect of Sentences

I ask students to analyze how different sentence lengths create varying sentence effects (see Figure 6.1). Again, I'll ask them to analyze just one paragraph, to keep it simple. I tell them that they are not limited to the effects I have observed—they may find new effects being created by different types of sentences.

SENTENCE	LENGTH	EFFECTS CREATED Emphasis, Choppiness, Slower pace, Faster pace, Suspense, Emotion, Conversational tone, or... OTHER!

Figure 6.1

Marking the Text for Sentence Effects

This technique leads directly into revising for effects. To make students conscious of the amount of sentence variety in an essay, give them a copy to mark up, and let them use their pens or highlighters to reveal the patterns. The specific instructions you give don't really matter—what matters is the experience of noting how the author used sentences.

For example, I might ask students to highlight each of the following in a different color:

1. Long sentences—Yellow

2. Very short sentences—Orange

3. Fragments for effect—Pink

4. Medium-length sentences—Leave white

Or, if highlighters are too much hassle:

1. Long sentences—Underline

2. Very short sentences—Circle

3. Fragments for effect—Double underline

4. Medium-length sentences—Leave plain

After marking the text, they can write in the margin what effects they think the author was trying to create.

WRITING USING SENTENCE EFFECTS

Getting students to be conscious of the sentences they write can be challenging, and my approach varies according to the student.

Drafting Using Sentence Effects

Some students can juggle many writing tasks at once: using details, choosing words well, not going off on tangents. For these students who can multitask as they write, I encourage drafting with sentence effects in mind. For some students, this comes naturally. I have found that students who are voracious readers have a tendency to use sentence effects without even thinking about it. However, if a student finds it overwhelming even to begin to think about creating any effects as he drafts, or if he tends to draft with a lot of clunkers, then he may want to work on sentence effects as he revises.

Revising Using Sentence Effects

When students finish drafting an essay, I will ask them to analyze it for their sentence effects, much as they did when reading, but this time they mark up their own text to find things that work and things to improve. Here is a suggestion for how they might do it.

1. Long sentences—Yellow

2. Very short sentences—Orange

3. Fragments for effect—Pink

4. Medium-length sentences—Leave white

5. Clunkers—Green

6. Similar sentences starters (e.g., "There was")—Underline

Once students have marked their own papers, you can give them a series of statements to complete:

1. I seem to have too many …. (short/long/medium sentences, clunkers, fragments.)

2. I like to use the sentence starter _____ too much.

3. I really liked these sentence effects I created: _____.

Marking up the text this way gives writers a very visual way to note whether they're using too many similar sentences throughout the essay or clumping them together in certain parts of it.

DELIVERING IDEAS

If ideas are the things we want to deliver to our readers' brains, our sentences are the vehicles we use to transport them. If our sentences are broken down, clunky vehicles with bad transmissions, our ideas won't be transmitting very well. We need to fix the vehicles if we want the ideas to go anywhere.

CHAPTER 7
Modeled Writing

One of the best ways, if not the best way to teach writing, is to write yourself. This does not mean that you write every assignment you give to your students (although I sometimes do write along with them, usually saving the results for use with later groups). It does mean that you should at least "keep your hand in" writing.

Over the years I have dabbled in essay writing a number of times; eight essays for the *Orlando Sentinel* over the past decade, about one a year, have given me a little portfolio of published writing to share with my students. They can see that I write for a real audience, for real purposes that are important to me.

SELF-ASSIGNED TEACHER WRITING: EDITORIALS AND COLUMNS

Over the years, I have written most often about our state's standardized testing program. My very first essay on the subject was about how my school at the time had made "A" level writing scores, yet been scored a "D" letter grade as a school for the year (1998). In 2000 I wrote a piece about everyone back-pedaling about the FCAT. Once scores improved, many of us in education began bragging about the improvement, thus jumping on the standardized-testing bandwagon. In 2007, I wrote the essay that appears in the introduction, the one that ultimately led to this book being written. So now I can really tell my students that you never know where going public with your writing is going to lead.

I have also written about my enthusiasms. In February of 2000, I wrote a tribute to the comic strip Peanuts as it came to a close after a nearly fifty-year run on the funnies page. Later in the year, I wrote a column in defense of the Harry Potter books. As a huge fan of traditional Disney animation, I wrote an essay titled "In Praise of Hand-Drawn Animation" to complain about their having closed their Orlando animation studio, but more to try to explain why I love hand-drawn animation.

All of these columns grew out of my enthusiasms or frustrations, or both. I keep a running list of possible topics for future essays. As I mentioned earlier, when we are discussing various topics around our house—educational, cultural, religious, political, or pop culture—and I get particularly vehement about a subject, my wife will say, "That sounds like a 'My Word.'" When we limit our students to canned prompts about gum chewing and school uniforms, we not only limit their ability to think like real writers, we are losing a vital chance to encourage them to think like real people, to be involved in life as public citizens and as private individuals.

STUDENT-ASSIGNED TEACHER WRITING

In addition to doing an occasional essay for the newspaper, I also let students take out their revenge on me for the standardized prompts I occasionally assign them. The game is called Prompt the Teacher. The day before we play it, I give students time to come up with a topic that I will be forced to write about. The rule is that they must be generic topics that could apply to anybody, just like the prompts on the real test. In other words, they must be fairly dull, but they can be fairly difficult. We list students' ideas on the board and number them. I then hand out scrap papers and students take a secret vote. Two reliable students tally the votes in secret and write the winning topic on a new sheet of paper. If I will be doing the writing in front of the class the next day, each of them keeps a copy and promises to be in class the next day. If I will be doing the writing outside of class and showing the results the next day, then they announce the topic and I write it down.

I have exactly 45 minutes, either in or out of class, to write my essay on the topic they assigned me. The catch is that they have to take notes on what I do as a writer.

METHODS FOR MODELING WRITING

The following methods for modeling writing apply to both a teacher's self-assigned essays like the ones I wrote for the newspaper, and to the Prompt the Teacher game. The idea with any modeled writing is to let students see the thought process you go through when you write.

When to Write

I do modeled writing one of two ways: outside class or inside class. Each one has advantages and disadvantages. Writing outside class works best, I think, if you are actually writing an essay for a newspaper. Writing outside class works best as well if you have large or poorly behaved classes. Writing inside class, in front of your students, is a challenging proposition. You have to be pretty confident you can pull off the act of writing, talking about your writing, and managing the class all at once. But if you can pull it off, the payoff is worth it.

Extracurricular Writing

When I write outside class, either for a newspaper essay or for a game of Prompt the Teacher, I save everything, either on paper or on the computer, so that every stage of my process is visible for students as I describe it. One advantage of doing the writing outside of class is that you can use the same example all day (instead of writing something new for each class). Outside writing can also be used as a series of mini-lessons at the start of class, rather than taking up an entire, exhausting class period.

When I model, I create a real prewrite outside of class, but as I adjust it and move it, I copy and paste a new version so that I can display for students the changes I've made. I then show this multidraft prewrite to my students on the screen in my room and discuss both how I brainstormed my ideas, and why and how I rearranged them.

When I drafted my FCAT Writing essay for the *Orlando Sentinel*, it was much too long. The *Sentinel*'s word limit is 475 these days, so I needed to do some substantial cutting from my rough draft word count of 748. After making the cuts, I used the two drafts side by side to show my students how I determined what to cut and how I tried to cut without sacrificing detail.

After I discuss my revisions with the class, I am ready to proofread. I let the class proofread the essay along with me. (I erase my corrections after each class by closing without saving, so that all the classes get to help correct the mistakes.)

If I am doing a Prompt the Teacher assignment outside of class, the process is largely the same: I get the topic from students, write on my own time, and then share with the class what I've produced. With a timed writing, I limit myself to 45 minutes, the same time limit my students operate under, but afterward I share a think-aloud of what I did as a writer.

Modeled Writing Inside Class

Writing in front of the class is not for the faint of heart—it's a bit of a high-wire act. I have seldom written "real" published pieces in front of the class. Usually I model a shorter piece of something longer—a paragraph, for instance—or else I will use the whole period and play Prompt the Teacher.

The advantage of modeling for the class is that the class gets to see you thinking on your feet and getting the job done within the 45-minute time limit. I project my writing onto the movie screen in my room so students can see the writing as it unfolds, and I talk them through my writing process as I compose. (More to come later in this chapter on projection methods and what to talk about as you model.)

From a classroom management perspective this is a challenging activity. To keep students involved and occupied, have them take notes. The notes are not about what I'm writing, but about *how* I'm writing—the kinds of decisions I'm talking about making as I write. Having students take notes is not just busywork. Rather it provides students with a record of the writing process to look over later. I ask them to keep their notes in their binders along with a copy of the finished essay.

Since I am concentrating on writing and on commenting on my own writing process, it's hard to watch the class. I try my best, though, and if it's a low-maintenance class, there are few problems, if any. If I know a class is prone to be talkative, I'll sometimes invite another teacher who has planning during that class, or a principal, to attend. Their mere presence can help keep students better behaved.

Technology

Obviously, some kind of technology is going to be required to make the modeled writing visible. It doesn't have to be anything fancy, though I have found that fancier is sometimes better.

Overhead Projector

Most teachers have the ubiquitous overhead in their rooms. It's handy and relatively low-tech. I occasionally model my writing directly on a transparency, but I find that the pens tend to be too thick, my writing too sloppy, and my pace too slow. If I am doing the modeled writing outside of class, I sometimes photocopy my actual handwriting, or a word-processed text, onto a transparency and use it to show my students how I wrote.

Computer Projector

Although I used overheads for years, and still use one occasionally, I now have a computer projector in my room . . . and I love it. I simply project my document directly onto the screen at the front of my room and start typing. Everything I'm doing appears neat and clean, and, if I'm writing in front of the class, in real time. If I project onto my dry-erase board, we can even mark up the text the way we would a real rough draft.

ELMO

If it's important to you to actually model using your own handwriting or printing for the kids, see if your school has an ELMO. An ELMO is like a traditional overhead crossed with a video camera. It projects onto the movie screen the image of whatever you place beneath it. You can view pages of books, pictures, or your own handwriting on a modeled essay. I do not have one of these devices in my room, alas.

THINGS TO TALK ABOUT WHILE YOU MODEL

However you decide to get your writing up in front of the class, it's important that you have things to say about it. Writing is not "invisible" the way reading is, since you can see the finished product of writing, but writing *process* is only partially visible. If all we see is a writer's final copy, then the writing process is not visible at all. If we can see a writer's plans, drafts, revisions, and corrections on paper, then the process is only partially visible, because we don't know what thoughts caused the writer to make those changes. Modeled writing makes the changes visible and the writing process transparent rather than mysterious.

There is an almost endless array of things writers do as they write, but certain types of drafting and revising techniques seem to be fairly universal and thus fairly useful to our students. When we model writing, we need to talk about our techniques and the choices we make when using them.

I think of this process as the inverse of the "think-aloud" that Jeff Wilhelm wrote about in *Using Think-Aloud Strategies to Improve Reading Comprehension* (2001). There the think-aloud technique was used to make the "invisible" reading process visible. I use it here to make the writing process visible. It is a form of metacognition. I am modeling for students not only what writers *do*, but how they *think*.

Writing is all about generating ideas and then making choices. When I model prewriting, I start by telling students how I am thinking of approaching the subject. If I am writing about a topic that I have chosen myself, I explain why the topic is important to me and what, if any, events led me to want to write about it. This explanation helps students see that writing doesn't exist in a vacuum—it comes out of our experiences and interests. If students have assigned me a generic topic, I explain how I am coming up with an angle on it that makes it uniquely mine. When assigned to write about a hobby, for example, I wrote about cartooning. I'm truly enthusiastic about it, and therefore the essay was as close as I could make it to being "real" writing. When assigned to write about a favorite movie, I tweaked the topic and wrote about the entire Star Wars series. Even with dull topics like "one change to make the cafeteria better," I talk about how I chose an angle that gave me the most to write about: add a Wendy's. Wendy's has a varied menu and thus a lot to write about. I also talk them through my brainstorming and ordering process: coming up with ideas as quickly as possible, then combining, trimming, and ordering them.

As I draft the body of the paper, I talk about how I make transitions, how I invent and add specific details and word pictures, and how I transition from one idea to another. I will sometimes stray from my outline, and I explain why am doing that as well—for instance, discovering as I write that an idea may not "work" or may work best in a different place in the essay.

For students who write to fill up the page almost without thinking, the amount of thought required is a real eye-opener. Even skilled student writers will come to realize how much they are doing unconsciously when they write.

When I model revision, I show how much fussing I do, especially over sentence structures. When I need to cut words to meet a maximum word count, my first line of defense is to cut "fat" in sentences, which often means tightening up sentences, which in turn often means cutting dead verbs and creating stronger word pictures.

Below is a reconstruction of what I talked to my students about when I discussed revisions to my FCAT Writing essay for the *Orlando Sentinel*.

WHAT I AM SAYING TO STUDENTS	WHAT THEY ARE SEEING ON THE SCREEN
This entire opening paragraph needs to go. It isn't a strong opening, and I'm sounding way too positive about the test. I don't buy in whole-heartedly. Also, it's not specific. I abandoned my original idea of starting the essay like a formula student essay—I didn't think my audience would know what to make of it out of context. They might just think I was just a bad writer.	This is not another essay complaining about the FCAT being too difficult, or being used to score schools. I am a Middle School Language Arts teacher, and I, quite frankly have bought into the writing test, with some reservations. I like the FCAT Writing test—at least the easy part. I could go on about the multiple choice section, but that's another whole topic. As head of my school's Language Arts Department, I get competitive about my school's scores, about my students' scores specifically. I get antsy as the test approaches, and I get positively jumpy as it gets time for the scores to be released in May.
I am going to make this paragraph my grabber/introduction, but it still lacks life. I need to create a specific scene: Last May when my school's FCAT Writing scores arrived, my principal hand-delivered them to my room. I accepted them with a shaky hand. As the Language Arts Chair at my middle school, I wanted us to do well. We did. A huge percentage of our students received the minimum 3.5 score. Even better, many received high scores: 5's and 6's, which are very difficult to get. This works much better. I also trimmed a lot of the information and made it briefer.	Last May, I was thrilled when our scores came out. A huge percentage of our students had passed the test with the minimum 3.5 score. Even better, we had a huge number of 5 and 6 scores, which are very difficult to get. Some schools don't get any 6's—we had about 15, and a whole slew of 5.5's as well.
I don't think I'm going to worry about insulting 3.5 writers. They may have tried hard, but the fact remains that it isn't very good writing.	My excitement over our scores turned a little sour, however, when I discovered that all of those high scores didn't really matter, at least not according to the state. All that matters is the number of students meeting the minimum standard of 3.5. Your school average does not affect the school grade. The number of high scoring students at your school does not affect your school grade.

Only the number of students meeting the minimum requirement. I do not mean to discourage or deride the accomplishment of students for whom a score of 3.5 is a major accomplishment, but a 3.5 is, quite frankly, not a stellar example of writing. The paragraphs usually begin with gripping phrases such as, "My first reason," "my second reason," and "my third reason," and the entire essay will sometimes end with a thought provoking "that's all I have to say about that": a la-Forrest Gump.

This paragraph works well . . . no changes.

But that 3.5 is all that matters, and it has a direct impact on instruction. If your school has to choose between having a lot of 6's or having a high percentage of 3.5's, it's going to shoot for the 3.5's. You shoot for a 3.5 by teaching a formulaic, five paragraph essay— the old hamburger essay. Have a main idea and three supporting details (in no particular order). Tell 'em what you're going to tell 'em; tell 'em; and then tell 'em what you told 'em. The hamburger essay may be a fine tool for many students, but for many bright students and enthusiastic writers, it is a cage.

In the interest of word count, I'm going to have to sacrifice some specifics here: the list of authors has to go. I'm replacing it with: You read published essays and drink in what good writing sounds like.

I need to do more cutting here. Adding the "hamburger" metaphor this late in the essay may not make sense to non-English teachers.

This is probably the place to end the essay, with making excellence part of the school grade. But it still isn't strong.

Here is what you do to get students to a 5 or 6. You don't worry about the "formula." You have your students read real essays: newspaper editorials, My Word essays, essays by an eclectic mix of authors: Anna Quindlen, Robert Fulghum, C.S. Lewis, Dave Barry, William Raspberry, among others. You teach them about organization and logic. Content dictates form, so essays may be anywhere from four to eight paragraphs—it depends on how many ideas the writer has. You teach students that there are many different organizational patterns, and that what works for one topic won't work for another. You teach them about the "showing" detail and the catchy turn of phrase. You teach them that writing is about having enthusiasm, about being engaged in the world and interested in what's going on around you. In fact, you spend very little time actually talking about the FCAT.

This final point needs to go, as I suspected in my prewrite. I didn't think there would be enough space for it, and it really doesn't fit. The topic of returning the essays to the students so they can read and learn from them deserves its own essay.

The new ending, "excellence is made part of the school grade" is weak. I need to make it stronger. Maybe I couldn't start the essay parodying the formulaic essay, but now that there's context for it, I could do a formulaic conclusion. Since I mentioned Forrest Gump earlier, I could end with "and that's all I have to say about that." But it needs context: How about . . .

I don't want to see them someday writing five-paragraph "My Word" essays that conclude, "And that's all I have to say about that."

That works!

Such an approach isn't "safe." There are still teachers out there telling your students that you can't even "pass" the FCAT writing unless you write precisely five paragraphs. I have had a student get a score of 6 with four paragraphs. When schools care only about the bottom line and the lowest common denominator, they will force teachers to play it safe: the five paragraph hamburger. Our students deserve to learn more than the minimal requirement, and that will happen a lot more if excellence is made part of the school grade.

One final note: the state does not release FCAT writing essays back to the students, I guess because of expense, and because a lot of people would challenge the scores. I have a proposal: release copies of the 6's back to the schools. It wouldn't cost that much, no one is going to debate or challenge a score of 6, and the schools would have the actual essays, not just the scores, to celebrate and to use as examples in the classroom.

The Power of Modeling Writing

Students need to see us writing. They need to hear what happens in our heads when we write. We, as teachers, learn how to teach writing better when we ourselves write and observe our own processes. We discover that real writing may take place in ways that are very different from the way textbooks and standardized writing tests would have us think. Modeled writing can show students how much thought needs to go into writing well, and how important it can be to write well if the issue really matters to you.

CHAPTER 8

Using Rubrics (or Not)

A few months back, Mark Lane, a columnist at my newspaper, the Daytona Beach *News-Journal*, took Abraham Lincoln's Gettysburg Address and applied the state writing rubric to it. Poor Abe came up short. Not enough word pictures. Too short. Lacked pizzazz. He would have failed and been forced to retake the test.

When I read Dave Barry columns, I often wonder how the Pulitzer Prize winner would rate on focus, as his essays digress in 60 directions at once.

I have been sending this book to my editor chapter by chapter. I am not writing to a rubric, and she is not sending me feedback based on a rubric. If she likes a chapter, I'm thrilled. If she's less than thrilled with a chapter, we are free to disagree about it.

She doesn't e-mail me and say, "Oh, on a scale of 1 to 6, that chapter is only a 2. Last chapter was a 5, though."

I don't e-mail back and say, "But I really think it's at least a 4. Couldn't we compromise and say it's a 3?"

That isn't the point.

RUBRICS—LIFE JACKET OR STRAITJACKET?

My basic premise through much of this book is that we should be encouraging students to act like "real" writers. With that in mind, I approach this chapter with some trepidation, because very seldom do "real" writers use rubrics. Yet rubrics have become a mainstay of not only our instruction and evaluation, but our very idea of what "good" or "effective" writing is. Rubrics are like writing prompts and standard five-paragraph essays: they seem like an easy solution, but they actually prevent students (and teachers) from having to think. I include this chapter on rubrics because it raises very fundamental issues about how we define, assign, and evaluate essays. But before I sound like I'm entirely slamming what has become a standard practice in many, perhaps most, classrooms, let me make an admission.

I am a rubric junky. If I claimed that I was above using rubrics, that I never went near the things, someone would eventually investigate the very computer I am typing on now. And they would find rubrics. Lots of rubrics. Rubrics for multiple grade levels. Rubrics for all genres, rubrics I've plundered from books and adapted, rubrics I've made up off the top of my head. I practically have rubrics on how to grade other rubrics.

They can't be all bad, can they? Well, no. But are they a life jacket, rescuing teachers and students from a sea of vague advice and purely subjective grading, or are they a straitjacket, tying us in to a narrow, mundane view of what writing can do or be that lets us avoid really thinking hard about our writing?

My thinking began to change when I read Maja Wilson's book *Rethinking Rubrics in Writing Assessment.* In it, the author challenges our current overreliance on rubrics. But I still use them when dealing with student writing—especially essays. Why? Well, they do have their good points.

The Good Points of Rubrics

1. *Rubrics are obviously useful for establishing what will be successful (or not) on a state writing test.*

I put this first because of its obvious (unfortunately) short-term importance to teachers and schools. I do spend some class time teaching my students to use the state rubric to score sample papers, and then to score each other's "timed writing" practice papers. It shows them the kinds of writing that get certain scores—especially the amount of detail. Many of my students look at sample of work considered "6's" from the state and say, "This isn't that good. I could do better!" I encourage them to do so.

2. *Rubrics give students clear criteria to evaluate their own and others' writing; without some kind of guidelines, writing seems like a mysterious, amorphous thing to many students.*

If you simply tell students to "write better," it isn't very helpful. A rubric can give students a helpful framework for thinking about their writing. It takes the vagueness out of the writing experience and gives them specific goals to shoot for in specific aspects of their writing. I can say to a student, "Your level of support is low—there aren't enough details," or "Your sentence variety needs work—they all start the same way."

3. *They can be versatile—you can make up rubrics of your own and make them as general or specific as you want.*

You are not stuck using only the state rubric. As I mentioned above, my computer hard drive has a rubric for every occasion. You can think about what "writing skills" you want students to demonstrate, and create a rubric that "fits" those skills. Specific rubrics can focus on genre conventions of a particular assignment, or on particular traits you'd like to emphasize. (More on this topic at the end of the chapter.)

4. *They create clear expectations before and during the writing process.*

When you hand out a rubric at the start of an assignment, everybody's clear about what the job is. You will be graded on these items, so make sure they are in your paper. However, this use of a rubric ensures that teachers are setting the agenda—not students.

5. *They make it easy to check on "learning objectives" or "instructional outcomes."*
In other words, they make it easy to grade essays, and to justify those grades. You can look at an assignment and say, "Here's what I was grading on: this, that, and the other thing. Here's how you did on this, that, and the other thing. Thus your grade is such-and-such." It makes grading less guesswork and more cut-and-dried.

6. *They are useful especially with beginning writers.*
Often inexperienced writers (and we do sometimes get them coming to us in middle school) have no idea where to even begin with writing. They don't set goals for themselves. They simply write to get the writing done with, if they write at all. Rubrics give them guidance on where to begin and what to aim for when they won't or can't set goals for themselves. So rubrics can be a great thing, supporting learning and streamlining grading. But anything that addictive has to have a downside.

The Problems With Rubrics

1. *They can get in the way of beginning writers . . . and stay in the way.*
I ended the list of "good points" by saying that rubrics were useful for beginning writers because beginning writers often don't set goals for themselves or expect much of themselves. If we want students to succeed at setting goals and expecting something of themselves, rubrics won't necessarily help, and may even hinder. As I've discovered, rubrics are habit-forming—for teachers and students. In the same way students get reliant on prompts and don't want to come up with their own topics, once students get used to your setting the goals via a rubric, they may not want to try setting goals for themselves. They will wait passively for the rubric and assignment to tell them what to write and how to write it.

2. *Rubrics do not necessarily encourage students to think deeply about their own purposes, writing style, and personal touch. They often write to "fit" the rubric.*
Rubrics can encourage a kind of laziness in student writers. You don't have to think deeply about why you are writing this or what will make it a good paper. Students write to fit the rubric, not to meet the particular demands of what they want to say. Rubrics can discourage independent thought much the same way the five-paragraph formula does.

3. *Rubrics often don't address accuracy of information.*

This is especially important if your school relies heavily on a state writing rubric. Our state rubric never addresses accuracy of information, and our "Directions for Writing" on the Florida writing test say that you may write something "real or imaginary" about the given topic. With no outside resources allowed on the test, we end up telling students to make up facts and statistics, as long as they sound realistic. "Seventy-five percent of high school dropouts live below the poverty level," sounds vaguely as if it might be true. "Seventy-five percent of high school dropouts get abducted by aliens" does not. However, both are fictitious. If all we teach is practice for the state test, using the state rubric, we are teaching students to make up facts. We have enough of that problem in some of our media outlets already—we don't need to be a contributing factor.

4. *Rubrics are not used in the real world of writing (so far as I know).*

I made this point above, but it bears repeating—in the real world, most people do not write according to the demands of rubrics. For specific job tasks or academic purposes, you may need to write highly formatted papers with very specific demands, but very seldom do those formatting demands take the form of a rubric. And when you are writing for your own purposes, a rubric seldom if ever comes into play.

5. *Rubrics encourage agreement, not differing viewpoints about writing.*

When I write a comic-strip gag I'm not sure about, I try it out on the family before I spend an hour drawing it. I do not hand them a "humor rubric" and ask them to rate it based on how hard they laugh. I see what works. I accept the fact that one person may think it's hysterical, a second person might not "get" it at all, and a third may not think it's all that funny. A rubric would ask everyone to "rate" the idea. If I treated a comic strip like a state writing test, I might demand that everyone in the house sit down and agree on a common rating—too much disagreement isn't "reliable." This would be a completely useless endeavor. What I want is the quirky, individual feedback I get from different people with different opinions. I can sift through the feedback and make my own decision, and sometimes the feedback results in my changing the gag to make it even better. "Rating" the gag would not produce any creative ideas.

6. *No rubric includes everything that is going on with a piece of writing.*
No rubric, no matter how comprehensive it tries to be, can really cover every aspect of writing that needs consideration. Rubrics may cover important aspects of the writing, but they may miss the nuances and subtleties that give writing its character. Rubrics limit our view of what a piece of writing can be, both as writers and readers. Even a program that is pretty comprehensive like "6+1 Traits" can't be all-inclusive. For instance, the trait of voice is used as a kind of catch-all trait for "focus on audience," "humor," "involvement with topic," "command of language," "connection with the audience," and probably a whole host of other hard-to-pin-down aspects of writing. Condensed down to voice and placed on a rubric, students may tell each other to "add more voice." How, exactly? If a rubric is our only lens for looking at a piece of writing, and the lens only sees primary colors, how are we to address the array of subtleties and shades of color that exist outside the rubric's spectrum?

7. *Many advanced writers may be doing things with their writing that are not on any rubric.*
We all have students who can go above and beyond what any rubric asks them to do—or who are just on their own strange, yet strangely valid, wavelength. Have you ever gotten the weird, funny, effective paper that just doesn't quite fit the mold—or the rubric? Last year I had a student take the clichéd topic "Explain why someone is a hero to you" and make up a completely bizarre superhero who "ate kitties and puppies for breakfast, but really wasn't a bad guy." It was hysterically funny, and completely on the topic, but I really don't know what an official scorer would have made of it.

WHEN TO USE AND NOT USE RUBRICS (TO RUBE OR NOT TO RUBE . . .)

If they have their good points, and they have their bad points, what's a teacher to do? Good question. I have been struggling with this issue for a while now, and I don't have any definitive answers. I'm quite a rubric junky, and it's hard to kick the habit. Are rubrics more useful the less experienced writers are, and the better they get, the more we can remove rubrics, like training wheels?

Or do rubrics merely become a crutch for everyone involved? The things that make rubrics appealing—easy to present, easy to write with, easy to grade—all seem to be on the surface of the writing experience. They make writing easy and clear, but for most writers, writing is difficult and complex—satisfying, even fun, but difficult and complex. Moving beyond rubrics takes us closer to what writing is really all about: making meaning and sharing that meaning with others.

Here is where my thinking has moved. Rubrics should be training wheels, not the bike. They should be the scaffolding you strip away so the building can stand on its own, not the building itself. Somehow they've become a permanent fixture when they should be an item for planned obsolescence.

Our goal, as always, should be to shoot for "real writer" behavior in our students. If we can use rubrics to nudge them in that direction, that is to the good. But as soon as we can, we should move them beyond overreliance on rubrics. This may be painful. Just as it's hard for some kids to let go of prompts and come up with their own topics, it's also hard to let go of the instant, ready-made expectations of rubrics and try instead to think hard about what you have to say and how you want to say it. But it is worth it.

But how can we let go of rubrics? They seem to have so many things going for them. Well, here are my suggestions. Take what you like and leave the rest.

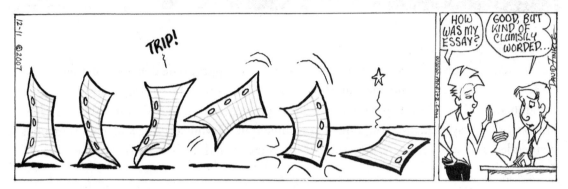

When to Use Rubrics

Are there times when you will want to use rubrics? Probably, yes. But we should think hard about which situations really call for them, and which don't.

1. *To get ready for "the test"*
I hate to lead off with this item, but if there is ever a time the rubric seems to be the be-all and end-all, it's on the state writing test. My eighth graders will take the test each February, and two years later they will take it again in tenth grade when it is a graduation requirement. They need to be able to pass it. Knowing how to write really, really well independent of the test will almost guarantee that they pass the test, but it doesn't hurt them to be familiar with the rubric and what sample essays at each score-level look like. It doesn't hurt, that is, as long as you make it clear that the test and its rubric are not the ultimate authority on all things writing, as long as you make it clear that they are artificial writing situations and artificial ways of looking at writing. It is a game they have to play, and they will want to play it well. But it shouldn't be the only game in town. Chapter eleven will have more to say about the test.

2. *To give students something to focus them as they evaluate, revise, and improve their writing*
For many writers, even adult writers, the decisions they have to make at every stage of the writing process can seem overwhelming. A rubric can help jump-start some writers by giving them a clear set of goals—but we must never forget that the real goal is to get them setting their own goals. A rubric can help some writers focus their efforts when they conference and revise—but we must never forget that our real goal is to have our students asking their own questions and making revisions to suit their own purposes instead of asking our questions and revising to fit the rubric better.

3. *To use in peer conferences*

Peer conferences can be a disaster when peers do no make appropriate demands of themselves or each other. Sometimes students will be too hard on each other, but in vague, insulting, and very unhelpful ways: "Your paper is stupid." More often, however, they simply gush over each other's work in ways that are nicer, but equally unhelpful. Having a rubric and a set of focused, open-ended questions can help bring some focus, honesty, and useful feedback to the table.

4. *To grade very structured, focused writing assignments*

There are times when, on the way to more independent writing, we teach our students specific writing skills and want to see if they are "getting" them. Designing an assignment that makes them use those skills may require a rubric so that you can see if they "got it." But this kind of assignment should be viewed as a kind of practice work leading to more authentic writing, not as authentic writing itself.

5. *To get students to think for themselves by creating their own rubrics—based on traits they see in other writers' writings*

When I was a budding cartoonist in school, I emulated Peanuts at first, but made up my own characters. Later, my writing and drawing style became more Garfield-esque. Later still, I began using more Disney animation techniques in my drawing, and then added a dash of Chuck Jones's Bugs Bunny style to the mix. My dialogue began to sound a little like Berke Breathed's Bloom County (now Opus). And all the while I was adding my own spin on things that eventually distilled it all down to my own style.

Emulation is not a bad thing—in fact, I think it's kind of an essential step most writers go through and possibly never completely get out of. Rather than giving students a prefabricated, generic rubric, pick an essayist you'd like them to emulate and after you've read a few essays, create a list of things that make Robert Fulghum essays or Leonard Pitts essays work. Have them generate the traits that make that specific writer work. Then try to write something using those traits.

Once you've done that as a class, you can have students try their own individual rubrics based on specific writers they admire. Even better, have them create rubrics that combine the traits of several writers they like.

COMPARE/CONTRAST ESSAY—RUBRIC AND SCORING

	HIGH 25 points	HIGH/MEDIUM 21 points	MEDIUM 18 points	LOW 15 points
Details/Word Pictures	Loads of details—overflowing	Quite a few details—full to the brim	"Enough" details—but not really "overflowing"	A few details, but mostly pretty sparse
Focus on Compare/ Contrast	This is clearly a comparison essay—two items are discussed in depth	Clearly a comparison, but may go off onto some tangents	Talks about two items, but focuses on one topic rather than both	Doesn't really compare two things—talks about different things
Clear Organizational Pattern	Very clear pattern—ideas are easy to follow	Clear pattern for nearly the entire paper	Pattern may be hard to follow—but we can tell what is happening	Facts about the two topics seem to be thrown together at random
Voice	This essay reads like a "real" essay—the author is involved in the subject and involves us, too.	This essay sounds completely like a real person wrote it, with only a few lapses into "generic" writing.	This essay gets the job done with some attempts at enthusiasm, but we aren't engaged all the way through.	This paper is a lifeless list of facts.
_____ **PRODUCT TOTAL** (out of 100)				

Figure 8.10

6. *To get all students to demonstrate a specific set of writing skills*

Let's face it, much of the time we assign pieces like persuasive essays and want all our students to write kind of the same thing, but with different topics and different points of view. I think it is a mistake (though one I sometimes still make), to simply throw a ready-made rubric at students, especially a generic rubric that could cover almost any type of writing. I am coming to the conclusion that if you are expecting similar, though not identical, things of all your student writers on a particular assignment, the best way to handle the situation may be to create a rubric together. If you've been reading essays that are similar to the one you'd like students to write, the task is even easier. Ask students to suggest what this essay should do. Say you are doing a "pet peeve" paper, students might call out, "Be funny" or "Use sarcasm" as traits the paper might have. You might wind up with a different rubric for each class period, and that's okay. Instead of handing them a ready-made rubric, you have made them think as a class about what is important to have in this particular essay. It's important that this happens each time you are asking students to do a particular type of essay. I am doing it for my eighth graders' "This I Believe" essays. I try to keep in mind, and ask students to keep in mind, that the rubric for a personal-topic persuasive essay (convincing the reader which restaurant has the best cheeseburger) may look very different from the rubric for a broader, more serious topic like persuading people they should not be eating cheeseburgers, or meat, at all!

7. *To make students evaluate their own writing according to goals they set for themselves when starting*

This is a kind of "neutral zone" between rubric and no rubric. You could ask students to set goals for themselves and create a rubric that would help them evaluate their own success. But you could simply have them set goals for themselves—and leave it at that. Every writer sets some kinds of goals for him or herself. Creating your own rubric is simply a more formal way to set your own goals.

Another "middle ground" approach is to do a kind of "half and half" rubric. Set some genre-related goals as a teacher, or as a class—certain traits that really need to be in every student's paper. But then leave the other half of the rubric blank—as empty boxes. Ask students to come up with some other, more personal goals for the piece. I did this with an assignment last year and it worked fairly well, except that several students had no idea how to set goals for themselves. This was a clue to me that I'd been using rubrics too much.

When Not to Use Rubrics

We have progressed from the very traditional state-exam rubric, out to the very edge of rubric-ness. Now we leave rubrics behind and enter the undiscovered country. When do you not use rubrics at all, and how do you get away with it? We begin where we left off. When do you not use rubrics?

1. *When you want your students to set their own purposes and criteria for writing*

This is really a segue from item 6 above. Ask students to set their own purposes for an essay. If you're concerned they'll go too easy on themselves, then talk to them about their goals before they begin. You can give yourself final approval of their goals, and you can prod them to challenge themselves more.

2. *When you want to get students to focus on their personal response to each other's writing, rather than on how it measures up to a rubric*

Rather than rating writing, why not simply look at what works for different readers and what doesn't? This seems like a rather obvious way of doing things since adult writers do it all the time, but somehow it seems too free form when we are dealing with students—especially middle school students who can be either gushy or vicious. On the other hand, it can be very exciting when students actually want to share with each other, simply because they are enthused about their writing and want feedback. Nothing pleases me more than to have students finish their drafts early and start to pass their papers to each other to read ahead of schedule, before the assigned conference day. Conferencing should be about that kind of feedback, that kind of excitement. Sitting and sifting your essay through a rubric seems like drudgery by comparison.

I'll have some ideas below on how to hold this kind of conference.

3. *When you want to publish their writing*

When you want your students to "go public" with a piece, your basic rubric could be "Ready to Publish" or "Not Ready." Publishing student work, which I discuss in depth in Chapter 12, adds a whole new element to the entire writing process. If an adult writes, he or she usually has a real audience in place, or else hopes to get one, and everything is aimed at reaching that audience, not on meeting the demands of a rubric. Another way to look at writing evaluation is this: is it ready for publication? If it is, then the job is done. If it's not ready, why not? Is it fixable, or are there inherent problems that make starting from scratch a better solution? If the essay is fixable, what does it need to bring it up to par?

Beyond Rubrics

Rubrics can help focus writing goals, writing feedback, and writing evaluation, so how do we accomplish these things without rubrics? We want our students to behave more like real writers, but they aren't there yet. How do we support them without doing all the thought work for them?

Getting Students to Set Goals for Themselves

When I write anything, be it a comic strip, an essay, or this book, I do start out with a kind of "internal rubric" in my head—an image of what I'd like it to be and do and say. It's a little different from a mere outline—it's less a list of content ideas than an idea of the kind of thing I want the writing to be. What's interesting to me, though, is that I often shift my internal rubric around as the writing progresses. I may find my focus is wrong and change it, or I may change my thinking completely as I write. I may realize that I need to substantially revise my inner rubric, so I do. You can't do that when the rubric came to you from someone else.

If our goal is to have mature writers who can set goals for themselves and give each other good feedback on how they are reaching those goals, we need some tools to use.

Students tend not to know what they want to accomplish as writers. They wait for us to tell them what their goals are. Asked what their goals are, most will reply "to get a grade," or "to get it over with." Ouch.

I am sometimes tempted to create a whole list of possible writers' goals, which includes things that are off the map of most rubrics—a menu of goals for kids to choose from. But that is almost as bad as a rubric. The moment you give them a list, most students think of it as a *complete* list.

So how do you assist them in creating goals, without actually creating the goals yourself?

Giving them "fill-in-the-blank" goals helps them invent and phrase the kinds of goals they wish to have. When I think of my goals as a writer of a given project, I have a whole host of things in the back of my head. Adapting those kinds of goals, but removing the specifics, leaves an open space for students to create their own goals.

Fill-in-the-blank goals might include:

- I want my readers to _____. (laugh, cry, get angry, feel comforted, see my point of view even if they violently disagree with me, think I am endlessly ingenious and imaginative. . . . The list is endless.)

- I would like to emulate _____. (Dave Barry, Stephen King, Kathleen Parker, or a specific essay by . . . . The list is endless.)

- I want to use certain types of details, like _____. (metaphors, similes, hyperbole, hypothetical situations . . . . Again, the list is endless.)

- I want to use certain writer's techniques, like _____. (circular grabber and clincher, logic, concealing my point of view till the end to create suspense . . . . The list is, well, you know.)

These goals may or may not match up with any rubrics, but they will be personal, meaningful, and more like the goals adult writers set for themselves. They are open-ended, and students can become independent goal-setters pretty quickly once they get the hang of it.

Getting Students to Give and Get Feedback Without Rubrics

As writers, we may want specific kinds of feedback about our writing. Usually I want confirmation that what I think is good is, indeed, good; I also want to know if the things I'm not sure about are any good, or if I was right to not be sure of them. My overall question is usually "Does it work for you?" not "What level on the rubric is it?"

If students have set their own goals, rephrasing them as questions is not usually a problem. Students can create their own conference questions based on their goals.

How did this essay make you feel, if anything? What effect did it have on you? Did it work for you?

Whose writing does this remind you of? (Who do you think I was emulating?)

What did you think of _____?

On the other hand, when students give feedback, they can be given tools that keep their feedback useful and constructive, rather than gushy or destructive.

For instance, when students read each other's papers, they might have different reactions to different parts of the paper. They might really like certain parts, not get certain parts, and find certain parts that they think need work.

You can work out a system with your students ahead of time, and create symbols that work for them. A plus sign might mean that the reader really liked something, a minus sign might mean that something didn't quite work for the reader, while a question mark might mean that the reader didn't get something or that they are questioning from the standpoint of agreement. Or it could be smiley faces, frowny faces, and "confused" faces. The symbols don't matter, or what they stand for really. What matters is they are giving each other real feedback about the writing.

With feedback like this, it helps to have small groups rather than pairs. After they've marked the papers with symbols, they can discuss the reasons for their marks. The author can take notes on the readers' concerns and sort out the feedback to decide what works for him or her.

Grading Without a Rubric

If I've made it this far without a rubric, grading will send me scurrying back for one. But I'm starting to get over that. There are other ways to grade, after all. And what is our goal with grading? I hope it is to improve students' writing. The problem with grading is that the second you have A, B, C, D, and F ratings, you have the makings of a rubric. That C must represent something like the same thing for all students, or you aren't being consistent, right? But writing isn't like other disciplines—it's not cut-and-dried. Students' essays are as different as the students who write them.

Nonetheless, most of us have to give grades. Here are some suggestions for grading that do not rely on a rubric, but will, I hope, lend themselves to improving writing.

1. Grade by use of the writing process

I usually give grades based on the writing process as part of a total grade anyway. Can students show evidence that they planned, drafted, revised, and proofread their essays? If, for instance, hardly any revisions were made, and there was no evidence of a prewrite, then points would be deducted. Really trying your best to plan your writing and later improve the draft through revision can earn a good grade, even if the final result was a bit of a failed experiment. (Rubrics do not encourage experimentation.)

2. Grade by number of finished, publishable pieces done in a quarter (portfolio approach).

I've seen this done a number of ways. Students can contract for a certain number of completed pieces for the quarter. Many portfolios also include a piece in which the student outlines his or her own areas of growth.

3. Is it publishable? How much remains to be done?

If our goal is to make students' writing "publishable," perhaps this criterion is most like the real world. Grades are assigned along a continuum such as this:

- Publishable, pretty much "as is"—A

- Needs a little work (could be quickly completed within class) on content and proofreading before being publishable—B

- Needs some work (needs to be taken home for additional time) on content and proofreading before being publishable—C

- Needs too much content and proofreading work to be considered publishable at this time. This is a paper in which the organization would need to be overhauled completely, or else the structure is there, but there is a lack of support, or too many mistakes to even begin to wade through—D

- Paper not completed—F

If a paper is in the C or B range, it can be resubmitted after further revision for publication, and for a higher grade.

What Writing Is All About

I know that the attempt to grade without a rubric described above has become . . . another kind of rubric. Whenever we give letter grades, there needs to be some kind of criterion. But I think we need to move beyond using a standard rubric for every assignment, and find more creative ways to evaluate student writing.

There may be other ways out there to grade without rubrics, and you may hit on a great way to do it yourself. Ultimately, our decisions say a lot about what we think writing is all about. Is writing a rote activity you do to get out of the way, or a real way to communicate with the world?

CHAPTER 9

Revision

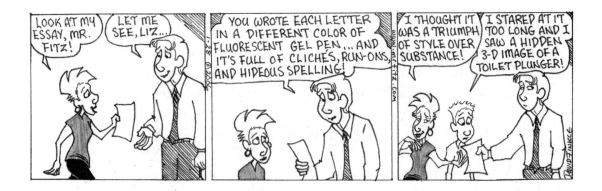

If there is anything student writers hate doing (more than prewriting), it's revising their writing. If there's anything they desperately need to do, it's revise their writing. Almost every book I've read on the subject emphasizes that writing well is about revising, rewriting, changing, and perfecting. Our students want to think their first drafts are perfect and leave it at that.

Students are also each other's "enablers." Often when we ask them to conference with each other about their writing, their comments are all gushy and overly complimentary. "Great job!" "Don't change a thing!" Or, like Ed Wood, the infamous B-movie director of *Plan 9 From Outer Space*, they simply write, "It's perfect!" They then approach your desk and say, "Suzie couldn't find anything to change! I don't need to do any revisions!"

CAUSES OF REVISION AVERSION

So, what causes this aversion to revising papers? Many teachers put it down to sheer laziness, and I have been tempted to do so myself, but I've slowly come to the conclusion that we may have, at least partially, created this problem ourselves.

Cause 1: The Test

Most state writing tests ask students to create a "writing plan" or prewrite and then spend about forty minutes writing a rough draft—no chance for revision or even much proofreading. If we make this test our goal for the year, our whole goal, we may wind up doing timed writing after timed writing. After all, why teach the writing process if it isn't tested?

Cause 2: Lack of Engagement

If you don't really care about what you are saying, internal motivation to revise is very low, and I have come to believe that revision is one activity that has to be internally motivated. I'm not going to debate the whole intrinsic versus extrinsic motivation conundrum here, but even if you think external motivators like treats, prizes, and points have their place, they simply won't work for this activity. If you are revising for a prize, the revisions you'll make are going to be superficial at best. You'll be revising to get the prize, not to actually make your writing better. Students will want to revise only if they care about their topics and their audiences. If they are only writing to dull, assigned topics, they will feel very little desire to get it right.

Cause 3: Lack of Audience

On the other hand, if they have something important to say, but feel no one is going to read their work, that's a motivation killer, too. Many student papers are never shared with peers, not even during the writing process. Some go into a "writing portfolio" never to be seen again. Many never actually get read by the teacher. We even have programs these days that purport to "score" writing without a human even reading it.

Writing should be about human connection. Even if students only get to share their writing in a small group or post it somewhere on a bulletin board for a day, at least it was seen or heard. Without some kind of audience, no matter how small, very few students will be willing to work hard on revision.

Lack of Revision "Know-How"

Many students don't know where to even begin to revise, just as I don't know how to even begin to repair my own car. I saw a cartoon some years ago, probably from *The New Yorker*, where a mechanic has opened the hood of a car, and is saying to the owner, "Well, there's your problem—it's an *engine*!" This is many students' problem with revising. "Well, there's my problem—it's a piece of *writing*!"

Many students haven't read enough good writing, especially good essays, to have developed criteria for judging their own writing. Everything just kind of looks the same to them. Students who read more have a better feel for what needs work to make it sound "real." That's why laying the foundation by reading good essays is so important. If you have no criteria for what a good essays sounds like and looks like, then you have no way of knowing what to change to make it better.

Viewing Revision as Fixing Problems

When I was given the chance to visit Disney's Orlando Animation Studio back when *The Lion King* was still in production, the animator who gave me the tour told me about a policy that the Disney artists had called "plussing." As animation drawings go from head animators to assistants to clean-up artists, each person is supposed to add to the quality of the drawing, make it even better. It isn't a question of fixing problems—it's a question of improving on already good material. I share this story with my students and tell them their approach to revision can be the same. Even if their paper is fine, they can "plus" it.

CONFERENCES THAT INSPIRE REVISION

Since "the writing process" became a kind of standard procedure in language arts classrooms, many teachers, myself included, have used conferencing to get students involved in each other's work, create a real audience, and inspire revision. As I've already mentioned, it doesn't always work. It is very easy for conferencing to become merely a formality. "Get these questions filled out quick so we can talk without getting in trouble!"

Using Rubrics

We discussed the good and bad points of rubrics in Chapter 8, but they are admittedly sometimes useful for conferencing, as they give students a place to start looking at the specifics of what works and what doesn't in a piece of writing. The state writing rubric can also be helpful in this respect. Some students need to know that *this particular* aspect of your writing is what you need to improve on.

Highlighter Conferencing

One fast way of conferencing without using a set of questions or a rubric is simply to use highlighters. This technique works especially well if you are looking at a very specific aspect of the essay. For the sake of simplicity, let's say you have two colors on hand, green and orange. But they could be any colors. There are several ways to use those highlighters.

Highlight for Organization

Highlight in green for topic one, orange for topic two in a comparison. You can quickly see how the essay is organized. Does one side get more attention than another? Is there a consistent pattern in the organization?

Highlight in green for the "pro" side of an argument, and orange for the "con" side. Are you consistently working against your opponent's arguments?

Highlight all the transitions to see if they are varied or all similar to each other.

Highlight for Word Pictures and Detail

Highlight any sentence that creates a picture or uses figurative language. How much highlighted versus nonhighlighted text is there? It should be mostly highlighted.

Highlight all strong verbs in one color and all concrete nouns in another. If there aren't very many, what does that tell you?

Highlight all "dead verbs" and adjectives with red or pink. Does the author need to use more active verbs or use more vivid details?

Highlight for Sentence Effects

Highlight clunkers in red. They need to be changed.

Highlight long, medium, and short sentences in three different colors. Are the colors all mixed up, or do all the sentences have a bland sameness to them?

Highlight any sentence starters that seem too similar to each other. Is there a good reason to start those sentences the same way, or do they need to be changed? There are many ways to use highlighters, and they make feedback on writing very visual and easy to interpret.

The Simple Revision Conference

If conferences are a place to get ideas for revisions, then one of the simplest types of conferences is one you can write on the board in your classroom in about a minute, then have students copy onto a sheet of paper and get to work using it in another minute. I call it the Simple Revision Conference.

Author_____ Peer reader _____

Essay title/genre _____

Keep?

Add?

Cut?

Change?

That's all there is to the conference. I have students write "Keep?" and "Add?" on the front and "Cut?" and "Change?" on the back, leaving plenty of space for response. The Keep section is what the peer reader really liked. He should give specifics: keep the organizational structure, keep these details, keep those great word choices, and so on. This keeps the whole thing from being an exercise in negativity. But the other three words give students very specific suggestions about what to add, what to cut, and what to change.

Student-Constructed Conferences

Although there is a great temptation to use a standard conference form each time students get together to look at each other's writing, there is a lot to be said for students creating their own conference forms. For one thing, we are doing a lot of the work for them when we give them a ready-made conference form. This may be a necessary step, but we want them to eventually arrive at a place where they know what kind of feedback they are looking for.

Many times, students' first attempts at coming up with their own conference questions are almost exact duplicates of what I have given them in the past, but as time goes on and they grow more confident, they begin to branch out (see Figure 9.1).

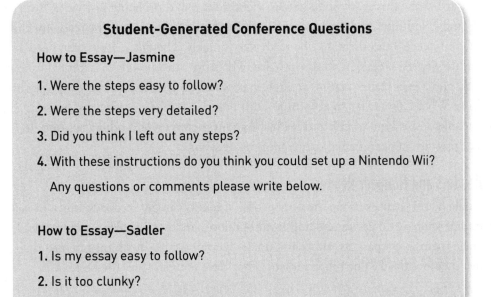

Student-Generated Conference Questions

How to Essay—Jasmine

1. Were the steps easy to follow?

2. Were the steps very detailed?

3. Did you think I left out any steps?

4. With these instructions do you think you could set up a Nintendo Wii?

   Any questions or comments please write below.

How to Essay—Sadler

1. Is my essay easy to follow?

2. Is it too clunky?

3. Are the steps well separated?

Figure 9.1

Open-Ended Conferences

When I look for feedback about a piece of writing, be it a comic strip, an essay, or a novel, I basically want to know two things: what works and what doesn't? I don't hand people a rubric for thrillers and ask them to rate my level of suspense, the vileness of my villains, and the level of psychological insight about my characters. I want to know their gut instincts and reactions. I want to know what they "bought" and what they didn't believe. Even when I get a lot of conflicting responses, they are all useful.

The open-ended conference is basically an invitation for conflicting feedback that the author then has to sift through and decipher (see Figure 9.2).

WHAT WORKS?	WHAT NEEDS WORK?

Figure 9.2

The open-ended conference is not a place to start doing conferencing and revising with students. If I threw this at my sixth graders right now, they'd probably just write "Everything works!" and "Nothing!" and be done with it. Some students may never be ready for this kind of conference, but others may be ready very quickly. The difficulty is, you need at least two mature writers to make it work—a writer who is mature enough to ask for this kind of feedback, and a peer reader mature enough to produce decent feedback to these very broad questions. What I always try to keep in mind is that this is where I want my students to end up—capable of this kind of talk and feedback about their own and others' writing. In Chapter 12, I address virtual open-ended conferences using wikis.

Peer Readers and Nonpeer Readers

I have talked as if their peers are the only people students can get feedback from. In fact, I encourage students to get second and third opinions, and not just from other peers. I encourage them to get parents, aunts and uncles, grandparents, or siblings to read their essays and give them feedback. The more audience they have that isn't me, the better.

Modeled Conferences

It is important to model conferencing. Even if students have been conferencing for a while, it helps to remind them what conferences are really all about.

I usually model conferences using one of four resources: a real draft I am working on, a "faux" draft that I have created to mimic many of the writing problems I am seeing in students' drafts, a real draft written by a past (anonymous) student, or a real draft that a brave current student really wants feedback on.

Depending on the source, I may copy a draft onto an overhead transparency and project it, or project it from my computer projector if I have a word-processed copy available. We then take a look at the essay and all give feedback. I encourage discussion and even civil disagreement about the piece.

For modeled conferences, I use whatever form of conference I am asking students to use, be it a rubric-based conference, a simple revision conference, or an open-ended conference. I want them to see how the document helps generate useful feedback.

REVISIONS

By the time writers have self-conferenced, peer-conferenced, and maybe gotten some feedback from a family member or from you, they usually have a pretty good idea of what they might want to change. Now it's time to actually begin the messy work of revision.

Practical Revision

Many middle school writers have no idea how to go about changing their writing. For one thing, they confuse revising with proofreading, and while there is some overlap, they are basically two different processes. I avoid the generic term *editing*, which blurs the line between the two. Many students will correct spelling and punctuation and call the changes revisions. I point out to them that correcting mistakes is proofreading, not revision.

Since so many students seem to have a hard time grasping what revision is actually all about, I give them practical advice about what revisions look like on a rough draft. Many students think revision means writing "Add more details here," somewhere in the margin and then forgetting to actually do anything about it later. That is not a revision. A revision is when you actually make the change!

There are many types of revisions to make, but only a few basic ways to notate them.

Clean Cuts

When my students decide they are going to cut something out of their essays, they pretty much decide they are going to obliterate, decimate, and completely annihilate those words. They mark through them with a vengeance. I tell them that if they are going to cut anything, a single, neat, straight line through the passage will do the trick. They may still want to read it later, either because they change their minds and decide to "undelete" it, or to see what they cut and why as a way of looking at their own writing process.

Margin Revisions/Between the Lines Revisions

Short additions or changes can be made very simply by writing things in the margins and using arrows to show where they go in the text. With a double-spaced draft, short changes can also be made between the lines.

Annotated Revisions

If students have more to add than a quick phrase or sentence, I advise them to put a number or letter on the page where the addition will go. On a separate sheet of paper, they then write the number again and write down the whole change as they want it to appear in the final essay. When they rewrite it or go in to make changes on the computer file, they can actually type that change in where it belongs.

One added note—although simply changing things on the computer is convenient, easy, and tempting, I encourage students to make hand-written changes on paper first. I think it is good for them to have a record of their changes to look back on, and quite frankly, it makes it easier for me to see how they've revised.

Circle and Move

Writers who decide to keep a sentence, phrase, or paragraph, but move it to a new location can circle it in its current location and draw an arrow to its new placement.

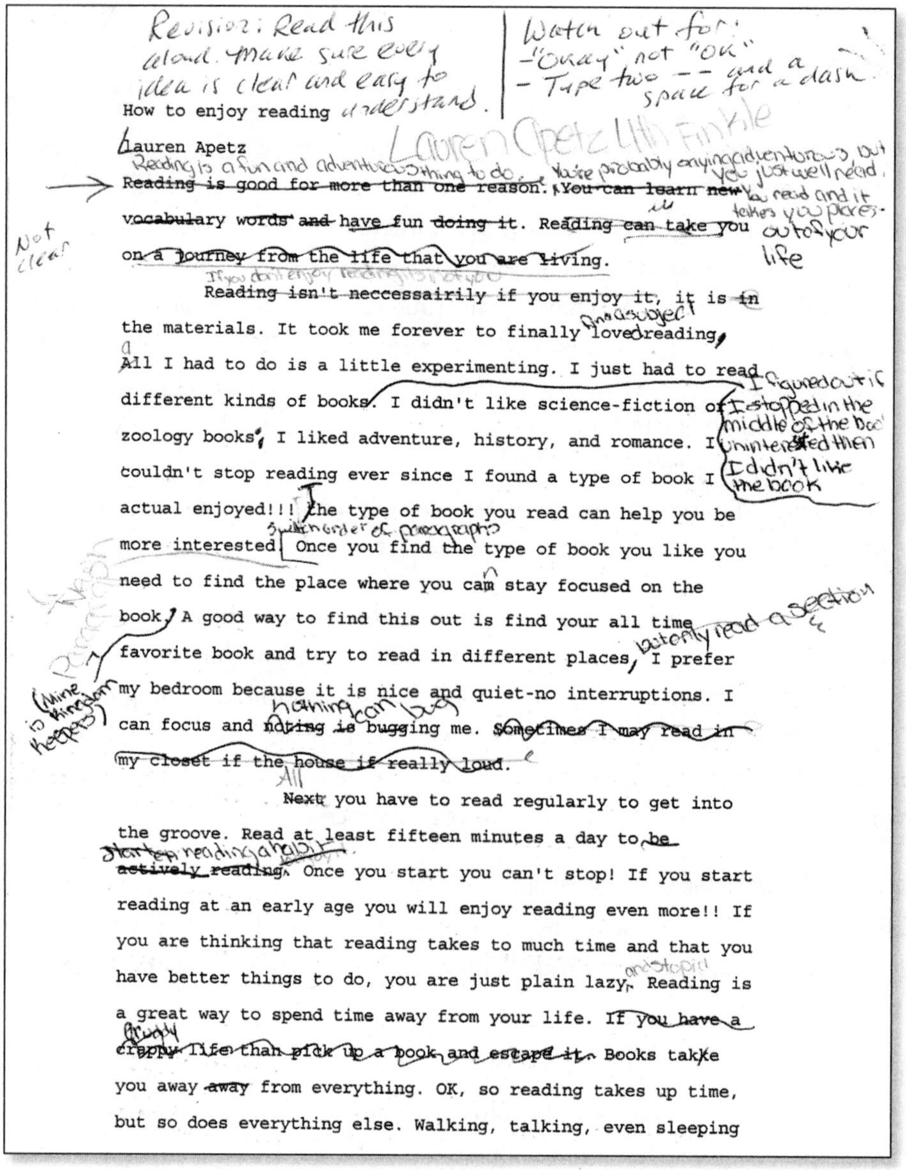

(Handwritten annotations on the top:) Revision: Read this aloud. Make sure every idea is clear and easy to understand.

(Top right handwritten note:) Watch out for: — "Okay" not "ok" — Type two -- and a space for a dash.

How to enjoy reading

Lauren Apetz *(handwritten: Lauren Apetz 11th Finkle)*

(handwritten inserted:) Reading is a fun and adventurous thing to do.

Reading is good for more than one reason. You can learn new vocabulary words and have fun doing it. Reading can take you on a journey from the life that you are living. *(handwritten notes: You're probably saying adventurous, but you just well read. to read and it takes you places, out of your life)* *(left margin: Not clear)*

(handwritten: If you don't enjoy reading it's in you)

Reading isn't neccessairily if you enjoy it, it is in the materials. It took me forever to finally loved reading. All I had to do is a little experimenting. I just had to read different kinds of books. I didn't like science-fiction or zoology books, I liked adventure, history, and romance. I couldn't stop reading ever since I found a type of book I actual enjoyed!!! The type of book you read can help you be more interested. Once you find the type of book you like you need to find the place where you cam stay focused on the book. A good way to find this out is find your all time favorite book and try to read in different places, I prefer my bedroom because it is nice and quiet-no interruptions. I can focus and noting is bugging me. Sometimes I may read in my closet if the house if really loud. *(handwritten notes: I figured out I stopped in the middle of the book, uninterested then I didn't like the book; switch order of paragraphs; but only read a section; (Mine is my bedroom. Nothing can bug me.); nothing can bug)*

Next you have to read regularly to get into the groove. Read at least fifteen minutes a day to be actively reading. Once you start you can't stop! If you start reading at an early age you will enjoy reading even more!! If you are thinking that reading takes to much time and that you have better things to do, you are just plain lazy. Reading is a great way to spend time away from your life. If you have a crappy life than pick up a book and escape it. Books takke you away away from everything. OK, so reading takes up time, but so does everything else. Walking, talking, even sleeping *(handwritten: Start a reading habit; and stupid!)*

Add

For many middle school students, writing enough text to create a full essay becomes an issue. They resort to a variety of tactics to make it look as though they've written more than they have and hope we don't notice.

If an essay simply isn't long enough, it's important to look at why. If the topic is focused too narrowly, there may not be enough to write about. That issue should have been caught when a student was prewriting and organizing. By the time you get to the revision stage, it may be too late to fix the problem, short of an almost complete overhaul. But assuming the topic has the potential to be a full essay, the problem becomes how to flesh it out without adding "filler."

Details and Pictures

If there is anything that is lacking in many student essays, it is the pictures, the pictures, the pictures. I'll ask students to get feedback on where readers had trouble "seeing" their essay. Where is more detail needed to make the subject vivid and clear and different for the reader? I then ask them to go in and reimagine how they could "see" their topic again. Could you show it through action? Through the senses? Through dialogue? Through figurative language? Adding just one or two more details to each middle paragraph sometimes vastly improves essays, and without a ton of backbreaking effort on the part of the writer.

Clarifications

If the author finds that people aren't getting what she is saying or are poking holes in her arguments, then sometimes it's useful to add clarifications. If an idea was a little fuzzy around the edges, a student may want to explain her ideas a little further or from a different angle.

Counterarguments

Sometimes a student writer will have addressed his own reasons for thinking as he does without ever addressing the opposing side's counterarguments. In other cases, he may have included the opposing side's counterarguments without really arguing against them. Some students fall into the trap of comparing the two sides of an issue without ever taking one. Some additional details or clarifications can help in this respect.

Cutting

For most students, the issue is writing enough. For some students, though, writing too much is an issue, and sometimes cutting can be even more painful than adding. I know this from experience. My 500-word essays for the *Orlando Sentinel* usually begin at 1,000 words, so I literally have to cut half the essay without cutting half the content. Knowing how to cut judiciously is an important skill that is often overlooked because we're pushing most kids to write *enough*. There is a great temptation to indulge the enthusiastic writer by allowing her to go over the word or page limit. I have almost always regretted this decision. Going through your writing with a fine-tooth comb to cut every word, every phrase, every sentence that isn't your very best writing can vastly improve it. In many ways, cutting is a more advanced skill than adding.

Redundancies

One of my high school English teachers, Mr. Jacobs, often told me I had sentences that came from the Department of Redundancies Department. Repetition to create an effect is one thing. Redundancy for no good reason should be cut, however. Sometimes redundant sentences are also guilty of circular reasoning. By the time you get to the end of a sentence, you've looped back around to the beginning again and said nothing. Encourage writers to cut to the essential meaning of the sentence.

Fat and Wordiness

As we saw in Chapter 6, some sentences have too much "fat" on them of "the reason why is because of" variety. Train students to go through and shave the "fat" from their sentences. Some students who start out with short papers will find they've said even less than they thought if they cut their fat, so cutting the fat out of a short paper may require the writer to go back in and add more "meat."

Unworthy Details

Sometimes students will throw in an anomalous detail that doesn't quite fit the spirit of the essay or doesn't support the main idea. Out they come. For instance, in the essay I mentioned earlier, complaining about the cafeteria's food, one student managed to slip in a sentence about how much they actually liked the chocolate chip cookies. Now it may be nice of him to say something positive about the cafeteria for once, but the middle of a tirade about food quality is not the place.

Anything That Is Not Absolutely Necessary

If a writer's cup "runneth over" with too many details, then it may be time to look at which ones go and which ones stay. I tell my students to consider all of the "deleted scenes" you can find on DVD's now. These are the scenes that the filmmakers simply had to cut for time reasons. The same thing applies here. Sometimes you have to "kill your darlings" as Dorothy Parker put it. Students who write a lot may need to learn how to choose the best details and shoo the rest away.

Change

This is the most subtle kind of revision—but it can be vitally important. Small, non-proofreading changes can have a big influence on a piece.

Audience Focus

If students are writing to a definite audience, age group, or person, it influences all aspects of their essay. I tell students to go through their essays and delete words or phrases that will offend or alienate their target audiences. If they are writing for a student audience, some slang might be appropriate, but writing for an adult audience might require more sophisticated word choices.

Word Choices

When students attempt to change bland word choices to more interesting ones, they sometimes go too far, commit "thesaurus abuse," and end up with overblown vocabulary.

Again, having a bank of words at their disposal is a good thing, and finding just the right words for the audience, the tone, and the topic is an essential aspect of revision. Modeled revising can give students a sense of how to make word choices, and of how important they are.

Details

Sometimes a detail may be almost perfect but need a little "tweaking." For instance, a detail might need to be a little more specific. I often tell children to use brand names if possible—not just soda, but Mountain Dew. The more specific the better, so long as it contributes to your main idea.

Some details don't fit the audience very well. In a timed writing, one of my students tried to convince the principal that the hallways should be made more spacious because then students could socialize better between classes without creating traffic jams. True, perhaps, but not a great detail for selling the principal on the idea.

Organization

Writers often begin following their outlines only to discover that what they thought was the best order for their ideas doesn't quite flow. They may need to shift whole paragraphs around and then change the transitions between them to make them fit. Transitions themselves may be an issue even if they are not moving paragraphs around. A lot of dull, repetitive transitions between paragraphs can break up an otherwise excellent essay.

Grabbers and Clinchers

Sometimes students may find that instead of opening and closing an essay with a bang, they've begun and ended with a whimper. The solution may be to head back to their notes and brainstorm ways to improve two of the most important sentences in any essay—the first one and the last one.

Clunky Sentences/Sentence Effects

Of course, one of the most insidious flaws in student essays is the awkward sentence. Changing them into sentences that flow can be taught (see Chapter 6), but students sometimes still need reminders to be on the lookout for them. They can also look at how all their sentences flow together.

While students are still getting adept at revising, I sometimes post a list of ways to revise in my classroom (see Figure 9.3). I also supply them with a checklist like the one below so that they can note or tally the kinds of revisions they have done on their drafts.

REVISION CHECKLIST (WAYS TO REVISE)	
Add	Details and pictures
	Clarifications
	Counterarguments
Cut	Redundancy
	Fat and wordiness
	Unworthiness
	Anything that is not absolutely necessary
Change	Audience focus
	Word choices
	Details
	Organization
	Grabbers and Clinchers
	Clunky sentences/sentence effects

Figure 9.3

MAKING WRITING THE BEST IT CAN BE

Our job is to help students realize that revising isn't the sign of a bad writer who doesn't know how to draft. Revising is the sign of a competent writer who knows what she wants to say and how she wants to say it. Students often lack both the ability to see what could be improved in their writing and the tools they need to actually make the improvements. If we can give them those tools, revising gives students a chance to play around with their writing and make it the best it can be.

CHAPTER 10
Proofreading

When I was in eighth grade, my teacher said, "We need to do our grammar unit." We all groaned.

"I know," she said, "it's awful, but we just need to get it over with."

What she meant, of course, was that grammar, as we knew it then, was an isolated skill you learned primarily by completing exercises out of a grammar textbook. You learned it, of course, so you could go on to fill out more exercises out of grammar textbooks.

Once this torture was over, we could get on with the real business of writing, like our eighth-grade short-story contest. I am proud to announce that I won that contest, and I still remember the whole story. Actually, I think I still *have* the story somewhere. I do not remember anything specific about those grammar exercises. And I know I didn't keep any of them.

I also think that my short story had a fair number of mistakes in it, mistakes we fixed by going over the story after I drafted it. I don't remember everything we fixed, but I recall learning a few new spelling rules, the correct format for dialogue, and maybe a rule or two for commas. That stuck with me.

All of this, of course, illustrates that grammar taught in a meaningful context is useful and meaningful. Grammar taught outside a meaningful context is, well, busywork. Teaching grammar in context is hard, though. It's so easy to assign exercises and check them off in the gradebook. You can point to them in your lessons. "There—I taught them some grammar, by George!"

PRINCIPLES FOR TEACHING PROOFREADING

But to look at students' errors in the context of their work is almost overwhelming. I try never to underestimate how bad student papers can be. That sounds awful, but when you get students who have made it all the way to eighth grade who have five mistakes on each line of text, it's easy to despair. Where do you even begin to hack your way through the tangle of problems? It becomes tempting to simply grade papers according to the official state writing test rubric and hope the problems take care of themselves. To actually sit and mark one of those papers can take 10 to 15 minutes, depending on the length of the paper and the frequency of the mistakes. Multiply even ten minutes per paper by 160 students, and you are looking at a total of 1,600 minutes to grade one assignment (which, by the way, comes out to over 26 hours of grading).

The worst part is, you spend 26 hours grading all those mistakes, only to hand the papers back to students and watch as they toss them casually into their notebooks or writing folders (or worse, on the floor) with hardly a glance at all your careful notations. So how to deal with this conundrum? Well, first, we need to have some principles to guide us.

Principle 1: *Students need to understand the importance of proofreading.*

Many students claim that proofreading doesn't matter to them. "The computer will correct everything for me!" "I'll just avoid writing for the rest of my life, and no one will ever know I can't do it!" "I don't care what people think—they shouldn't judge me by my writing."

When comments like those start to fly around the room, it's time to be subversive. One way to get them to admit that proofreading matters is to catch them off guard. Read the first couple of "Progris Riports" in the short story "Flowers for Algernon" and ask them what they can tell about the writer. Polite students will say he isn't very bright; less polite students may call out something less tactful. If your state releases anonymous essays from the state writing test as Florida does, show them examples of low-scoring papers. Discuss them with the class— listen to their reactions. I have never had a student say, "Well, they made a lot of mistakes, but it's okay!" Invariably, they disparage the mistake-riddled writing. Sometimes students who make the most mistakes in their own papers are most vehement in condemning other people's mistakes!

I ask students for their impressions of these writers, and they nearly always say that the writer either isn't very smart or didn't care enough. The point isn't to pick on poor Charlie Gordon or the low-scorers on the state test, but to show students that their own gut reactions show them how important correctness is.

We return to their "Why Write?" notes from the beginning of the year and look for types of correspondence that must be hand-written, where the computer is no help. We look at errors that the computer can't help you with. I have seen three student papers this week alone where careless use of the spell-check lead students to replace a misspelling of "definitely" with "defiantly." The effect is humorous ("I am defiantly going to start doing my homework!") but not intentionally so.

Principle 2: *Students need assistance in learning and retaining some of the basic rules of grammar; they will remember these rules better if they are taught in context.*

I use the phrase "in context" to mean "anything that is not in isolation." Obviously, teaching grammar during a one-on-one editing conference is "in context." But so is teaching a mini-lesson on a certain skill a lot of students are having trouble mastering. I would argue that teaching grammar as part of an ongoing serialized story as a "bell-ringer" activity is a meaningful context. If students can relate it back to their own writing, it is "in context."

Principle 3: *Proofreading activities need to happen mainly before the final copy is turned in.*
Once a paper is turned in, it's dead. By the time you've taken a week (or more) to grade that paper with its other dead compatriots, it is buried. By the time you turn it back to the student with comments on it, your comments are the paper's obituary.

The only exception to this principle is when you are the final-copy editor and students need to go back into the piece and make further corrections on it—especially if those corrections are for publication.

Principle 4: *The task of proofreading should fall mainly on the student, not the teacher.*
If you have to use up an entire colored pen on a single essay, you are allowing for too many mistakes. It's time to hand the paper back to the student, give her any assistance you deem necessary, and set *her* to work on correcting it.

Principle 5: *Many students will be intrinsically motivated to proofread if they care about their topics and feel there is potentially a "real" audience other than the teacher.*
I realize that some students seem to be completely unmotivated—intrinsic, extrinsic, it doesn't matter. Nothing seems to work. But I really do believe that most students will want to correct their mistakes if they really care about the writing and know it may be going before a real audience.

With these principles in mind, we'll take a look at how to decide which kinds of errors and corrections to teach and ways to teach proofreading, both to a class and to individual students.

DIAGNOSING PROOFREADING PROBLEMS

After you've established why proofreading matters, it's important to figure out what proofreading problems to address. Many of the subjects covered by grammar texts don't even address proofreading problems directly. For instance, many texts cover interrogative, declarative, imperative, and exclamatory sentences. The only time I've ever had to address any of these types of sentences in relation to students' actual writing is to explain why an imperative sentence (*Wash the car!*) isn't a fragment. We'll talk about the subject (You) being implied rather than stated. Other than that, I don't much see the use of covering those structures.

I like to give a "diagnostic" piece of writing near the beginning of the school year when I get new students. It will give them a short, very open-ended topic and ask them to keep it brief—half a page to one page. I will sometimes give them a list of things it must include—for instance, a list written as a sentence, or people talking to each other using quotation marks.

I warn students before they begin that this is one paper that I will be marking up completely for every single little mistake. To prevent casual sloppiness about mistakes, I may challenge them to make their paper mistake-free for extra credit or a treat. It's hard to tell what they really know if they aren't really trying, and some students will do just about anything for extra credit or a treat.

Correcting these papers isn't hard, especially if you put a time and length limit on the writing, and you find out a lot about what your students are having problems with.

All-Class Problems

To find out about problems that whole classes are struggling with, I will sometimes mark "error symbols" in the margin of each paper, so I can easily see *RO, FR,* and *Caps* listed down the side. I will then tally up these types of errors for an entire class, or for all my students, with hatchmarks on a separate paper to see which errors are being made by many students (see Figure 10.1).

TYPE OF ERROR	FREQUENCY IN THIS CLASS
RO's	////
Frags	~~////~~/
Homonyms	//

Figure 10.1

By the time I'm done with this process, I have a pretty good idea of what mistakes a lot of my students are having trouble with, which helps me focus my all-class lessons.

Individual Problems

In the course of tallying up, I may find some students have particular problems that most others don't. It's important to note these students and their mistakes, because they offer you a chance for some powerful one-on-one instruction later.

Students whose mistakes are "off the beaten path" tend to come in two varieties, struggling writers and advanced writers.

Struggling writers tend to commit everybody else's mistakes, but they also commit mistakes unique to them. Usually a struggling writer's mistakes tend to be "remedial" in nature. While the rest of your class may be spelling most "commonly used" words right, these students may still be mixing up *were* and *where*, or using invented spellings that don't quite make sense. They may be using uppercase and lowercase letters incorrectly, or jumbling them together inappropriately. They may simply not use end punctuation. If this is the case with some of your students, they are going to need extra help, separate from the rest of the class. Getting them that help may prove problematic, however, since students themselves may be embarrassed about the problem. (More on how to give individual students help later in this chapter.)

Advanced writers, on the other hand, tend to avoid many of the common pitfalls of their classmates—no run-ons, comma problems, or misspellings. Instead, they are committing more sophisticated kinds of errors that aren't even remotely on other students' radar yet. They are messing up their parallel structures; they are using semicolons, colons, or dashes incorrectly; they are stumbling when they attempt complex sentence structures. These students also need some individual attention, and any all-class instruction you do will be a review for them.

Rules Worth Knowing

Seeing what kinds of mistakes your students are making helps focus your efforts. Obviously, if over half your students are creating lots of run-on sentences or comma splices, that topic will need to be addressed.

Now, my goal here is not to provide an extensive grammar handbook. There are plenty of those in grammar textbooks, writing textbooks, literature textbooks, and various adult and student handbooks. I do want to discuss our approach to teaching these rules.

First, I try to avoid technical jargon whenever possible. I only use technical terms like *gerund*, *infinitive*, *participle*, and so on, if it becomes necessary to explain how to correct a certain mistake. Second, I focus on problems and solutions, not on isolated analysis of concepts, such as identifying parts of a sentence—unless the analysis helps to solve the problem.

For instance, I do teach subject and predicate, because analyzing a sentence for their presence clues you in on whether you have a sentence on your hands, or a nonsentence such as a run-on or fragment. That's useful. Now almost any term may become useful eventually, but until you actually need to know it to improve your writing, you don't need to know it at all, because it is unlikely you will remember it.

What errors do I find my middle schoolers struggling with most? The list probably looks familiar to you: run-ons and fragments, comma use, apostrophe use, quotations and dialogue formatting, pronoun usage with compound subjects or objects ("Me and her went to the store."), adjectives and adverbs usage ("You did good."), and spelling rules and their exceptions. That actually isn't a very long list, and those problems probably account for 90 percent of the mistakes I see. If you can teach them to eradicate those types of errors, a lot of the battle is over.

But how do you teach them to eradicate them? I use two approaches: whole-class and individualized.

All-Class Proofreading Instruction

The first rule of whole-class grammar instruction is that it should never last more than ten minutes. After ten minutes, students tend to have two diametrically opposed and equally "off-task" reactions. They either fall asleep or become very, very agitated and begin to throw things.

The second rule of whole-class grammar instruction is that it should be perceived as useful to students. Giving a grammar lesson while you aren't even writing anything at the moment isn't going to seem terribly relevant. Giving a grammar lesson about dialogue and quotations as your students are struggling to use dialogue and quotations in a narrative essay, on the other hand, is very relevant.

Proofreading Mini-Lessons

Students need to know three things:

- Why is something a mistake?
- How is it supposed to look?
- How do I fix it?

When I present a proofreading mini-lesson, I usually find examples from old student papers, make some up myself, or else take textbook examples and tweak them. Textbook examples are nearly always boring: "Jane gave her apple to George he took it gladly." Find your inner Gary Larson (creator of The Far Side comic strip). "Jane-bear gave her piece of the hunter to George-bear he took it gladly." I have sometimes let students revise textbook exercises for me to make them more interesting, and I must say, the results are always . . . interesting. Not always usable, but interesting.

At any rate, we always look at the example at hand as if we'd found it in a real paper we were proofreading. First, we discuss why something is a mistake. I ask students to explain it. "It's a run-on, because there's a subject and predicate and then another subject and predicate, and they aren't linked or separated."

How is it supposed to look? We discuss this question as well, and realize that sometimes there is more than one right answer. "This should either look like two separate sentences or like one big, two-part sentence linked together by something. It can't just be one big sentence with nothing holding it together."

Lastly, how can we fix it? "Either we separate it with a period where the first sentence ends, or we join the sentence with a comma and conjunction or a semicolon."

This basic approach of asking the three questions applies to any proofreading problem you may encounter, and it does not require that you use complicated terminology for its own sake.

The Grammar Story

This three-question approach can be used with another type of mini-lesson: the serialized grammar story. Pioneered by Jane Bell Keister in her Caught'ya books, this approach uses a series of grammar lessons that tell a story. When students enter class, they spend five minutes copying down a mistake-riddled section of an ongoing story. When the five minutes are up, the class reviews the mistakes, discusses how to correct them, and moves on to the lesson for the day.

If the story is interesting, students will want to see what happens next. In her books, Keister encourages teachers to come up with their own proofreading stories, so of course I did so. I wrote a story called "Genre Jumpers," about book characters that discover their own fictional nature and chase a villain, the Grammar-nator, from book to book. The Grammar-nator is creating mistakes in every book and it is up to the readers (my students) to stop him. I can focus individual episodes on particular mistakes I see my students making, and students have fun guessing what is going to happen next.

Another advantage is that I can circulate around the room as my students work and check out if students are making the corrections for themselves. In a couple of episodes, they have to save a character's life by correcting an error a certain way.

For example, in a western book, the Grammar-nator has sent an "eraser ray" at the town sheriff, the man in white:

The beam abruptly terminated the man in white, the sheriff fell in a heap!

This is a comma splice, but it can be corrected in such a way that if they place the period correctly, the beam terminates, not the sheriff. The sheriff faints, but doesn't get erased.

The beam abruptly terminated. The man in white, the sheriff, fell in a heap!

I walk around saying, "You saved him!" or "No—he's still dead." Saving a character's life is very motivating.

HOW TO TEACH PROOFREADING INDIVIDUALLY

Many errors can be eradicated simply by doing some shared exercises. Some repetition is important. But students almost always need individual attention on their actual writing, especially those struggling or advanced writers I mentioned earlier. If marking errors and returning papers doesn't work, what does? It depends on your situation. Class size, class make-up, and class level all influence what approaches you can use, but here are some suggestions.

Galley Proofs

A galley proof isn't a final copy—it's the last version of a text that gets proofread before a book goes to press. When students write "final copy" on a paper, it's all over. By calling what they turn in a "galley proof," they realize the piece isn't finished, and that there is still work to do. After you've looked over the paper, they will still be doing their final copies, where their job will be to fix the remaining problems. After all, an author doesn't write a book or essay in hopes of stopping when the paper is all marked up with an editor's ink.

Proofing Short Pieces

Especially early in the year, I will assign some very short, one-paragraph pieces of writing that are not full essays—more like letters to the editor. It is much easier to proofread a half-page paragraph than to go over an entire multiparagraph or multipage epic. I can usually have a paragraph proofread and back to students the next day for them to do a final copy. Try to work out some of the major issues on short pieces before moving on to longer ones.

Circling and Revisiting, Not Correcting and Handing Back

Instead of actually using any editor's marks or making any corrections, simply circle or highlight mistakes. Don't give any explanation, unless the mistake is one that you've never addressed in class. Hand the paper back and ask writers to do the work of figuring out what's wrong and correcting the mistakes—and give them a deadline.

Returning Unmarked

With some students, especially ones who know how to proofread better than this particular assignment would indicate, I will simply hand their paper back with "Proof over!" written across the top. If I feel it might help, I may write a quick note about what kinds of errors they are most guilty of at the top. "Proof for RO's!" "Proof for SP!"

I expect them to use that day's writing time to make the corrections, or else to make them for homework and return it the next day.

Proofreading on the Run

Proofreading on the run is exactly what it sounds like. I move around the room, glancing over students' papers as they finish their "galley proofs" and look for mistakes. I'll skim over a paragraph or two, point out one or two types of mistakes I'm seeing, and tell them to check the rest of the paper for that type of error. I then circulate some more, and return to that student later to see how they've progressed.

This technique is especially useful if students are word-processing in a computer lab. I can look on the screen and find mistakes very easily, and sometimes actually commandeer the keyboard for a moment to show them how to make a certain correction. I then set them to work finding more mistakes of that kind, and go talk to other students.

Proofing Pass-Around

Put students in small groups, preferably of four, and have them pass their galleys from person to person to hunt for mistakes and help each other correct them. A great tool for this activity is erasable colored pencils. Students can each mark errors in a different color, and if the proofreaders make mistakes in their proofreading ("Oops! You *did* spell *facetious* correctly!"), they can always erase them. Meanwhile, you can circulate, observe, comment, settle debates, and assist.

Using Student Proofreaders

You may occasionally have students who have mastered most major proofreading skills and who finish their papers early. I will sometimes make these students into apprentice editors. They can edit on the run and troubleshoot for their fellow students. I offer extra credit if they do a good job at it. Of course, teaching something helps you learn it better, so this activity also solidifies their skills.

PREPARING FINAL COPIES

Sometimes I will use more than one of these techniques: proofing on the run in class, small-group peer proofing, followed by proofing on the run in the computer lab. After the papers come in to me, I may hand them back for students to check over one more time and resubmit. But in the end, I ask them to create a final draft that is practically error-free. The main thing is to get students working more on their own proofreading issues, and you working less. They need more practice with proofreading than I do.

CHAPTER 11

Tips for the Test

I have been teaching in Florida, on and off (mainly on), since 1990, shortly before they introduced their standardized writing test in 1992. The standardized writing test has been an undercurrent for my whole teaching career, which is a scary thought. I have very, very mixed feelings about the test.

In 1993, the average score for eighth graders was a 3. This, quite frankly, astounds me. A 3 on the Florida rubric is not exactly a ravishingly good piece of writing. For a long time, getting students to rise to the level of formulaic drivel was the driving force in Florida education. Formulaic drivel was, I suppose, better than doing no writing at all. But not much better, I've since decided.

We have now reached the point where nearly all of our students pass at the 3.5 level, and the vast majority receive a 4, which means they can write a not-great-yet-not-dreadful rough draft in 45 minutes about a topic they may or may not have any interest in. So the teaching of writing has improved since I started teaching—at least on paper (pun intended).

But I worry about the effects of the test.

Almost without your thinking about it, Test Day becomes the central day of the whole school year in eighth grade, the year they take the "FCAT Writing" in Florida. Everything either leads up to the first week of February or leads away from it: a bottleneck of tension followed by a period of educational creative freedom. As I wrote in my essay for the *Orlando Sentinel*, I wait with bated breath for the scores to arrive. We count our "perfect 6's." We crunch our data. We compare ourselves to the other schools in the county. We give certificates to our high-scoring students. Despite ourselves, we start to act as if it really is all about the test.

It doesn't have to be all about the test, and it shouldn't be all about the test.

Here are some questions to ask yourself about your school, your curriculum, and your classroom.

- Do our students write about what matters to them, or only to "test-prep" prompts?
- Do our students write in multiple genres for multiple audiences, or only to the genres included on the test?
- Do we shoot for the best possible writing or the minimum passing score?
- Do we encourage students to love writing, to make meaning, to grow as people through writing—or do we just encourage them to pass the test?

- Do our grading and evaluation really look at students' papers in depth as the writing of individuals who have important things to say, or does our grading mainly consist of scoring papers according to the state rubric?

- Do we encourage students to prewrite, draft, and then engage in the messy and difficult task of revising and maybe publishing their writing somehow, or do we stop at the rough draft nearly all the time, because the test is only a rough draft?

- Do we teach them how to really think about their ideas and organize their writing a variety of ways, or do we teach them to write to a formula because it's safe and will get them a passing score?

- Do we talk about real-life reasons why people read and write, and encourage them to write for those reasons, or do we use threats, pleading, pressure, or bribery to get them to pass the test because the test is all that matters?

We all need to ask ourselves, to use a cliché, whether we are putting the cart before the horse. I include myself in that statement. There is something Faustian about the promise that if you can just get all your kids to a passing score on a test lasting 45 minutes, then you have done your job as a teacher and nothing else matters. We must fight temptation.

Good writing for real purposes must come first; the test should be an afterthought. When I was a student, that's how it was. The standardized tests were never talked about. They arrived one day, we took them, we forgot about them, and later we got our scores. There were no school grades, no graduation requirements based on test scores, no third graders throwing up the morning of the test because not passing might lead to repeating the grade. I bring up this rosy past not to pine away for it, but to suggest that we might want to start emulating it, despite all the pressure to emphasize the test. Maybe we should talk less about the test and more about why students are really learning.

Here is the approach I've adopted: I repeatedly emphasize why reading and writing are important for all kinds of practical, professional, and personal reasons. (See Chapter 1.) I talk about how reading and writing can change your life for the better. We work on real writing improvement, not test preparation. I mention the test as little as possible.

But in the end, I *do* mention the test. The test is how our school's grade and funding are determined. The test, whether I like it or not, matters. It is also true that some of the writing our students will do in the real world will be similar to the state test because of a standardized topic, a time limit, or both. College entrance essays; job application essays; scholarship essays and writing contests; and on-the-job writing assignments such as reports, brochures, and articles are all written to a kind of prompt. Many of these types of documents are also written on a time limit. So when I do talk about a test, I try to emphasize the ways in which it most closely resembles something they will have to do in the "real world."

With the idea that the test is not the driving force of a writing program, and assuming you have taught them to be good essay writers for "real" purposes, here are some pointers for getting students to succeed on the test.

ANALYZING THE PROMPT

Your state prompt probably follows a certain format. It's important to give your students some familiarity with the format of the prompts they will see on the test, and it doesn't take long to do so. In Florida, we always get a booklet with sample essays from last year's test, but it never gives you the exact wording of the prompt—only a paraphrase of it. It's pretty easy to discern what the wording on most of them would be, however. The Florida prompts always have the same two sections: Writing Situation and Directions for Writing. Usually they read something like this for an expository prompt:

> WRITING SITUATION: *Most people have certain times of the year they like better than others.*
> DIRECTIONS FOR WRITING: *Explain why you especially like one certain time of year.*

Or this, for a persuasive prompt:

> WRITING SITUATION: *There are many ways in which communities can be improved.*
> DIRECTIONS FOR WRITING: *Convince your community's leaders to accept your suggestions for improving your community.*

These topics are always terribly generic, so that they can apply to anyone without bias. Giving students a chance to get familiar with the type of wording also gives you a chance to teach them to do a little analysis of these prompts, and despite their simplicity, analysis is necessary.

The Audience

Of all the mistakes I will see on my students' prompted writing, addressing the wrong audience is number one. I sometimes give a prompt that tells students to persuade a friend not to drop out of school. Many of them write something along these lines: "My friend told me they were going to drop out, and I told them not to." They are writing *about* their friend, not *to* them. I emphasize to students that in nearly every prompt they are given a fictitious audience. They need to identify that audience if it is mentioned in the prompt, and write to that audience throughout the entire essay.

Real Writing Application: Focus on your audience is an important rhetorical concept; audience influences all your decisions as a writer: details, word choices, even organization.

The Genre

As in most states, Florida middle school students write in one of two modes, persuasive or expository. It is important that students be aware of which genre they are asked to use. For persuasive, the key words are *convince* or *persuade*; for expository, the key words are . . . *explain*. Okay, so there's only one key word for expository. This may seem too simple to even mention, but some students don't concentrate on genre if we don't point it out, and the result can be an out-of-focus essay. I have seen students take a persuasive topic, whether to have school uniforms or not, and turn it into a comparison paper that never takes a side. "Some people say school uniforms are bad, some say they would be good. Here are their reasons." That's not persuasive.

Real Writing Application: Students do need to be aware of the genres they are writing in, especially when they are allowed the freedom to choose their own topics and genres. They need to give thought to what genre best suits the topic they've chosen.

Topic and Focus

Students need to be sure to read the prompt carefully. I tell them to look for singulars and plurals. Does it ask for "one change" that would make your school better, or "changes"? This distinction could change the entire structure of your essay. Are you writing about one change with several reasons why the change would be beneficial, or are you writing about several changes in less detail?

Students also need to be careful, as they prewrite and write, that they don't go off on a tangent. A prompt asking students to explain their favorite thing in nature can easily turn into a narrative about a family camping trip that only peripherally mentions the writer's favorite thing about nature.

Next comes something I absolutely hate to tell them but in fairness feel I must. For the sake of the test, they should not necessarily argue for the side they really believe in: they should argue for the side that is easier to write about. They only have 45 minutes. This writing will never go before a "real" audience. They need to make it as easy on themselves as possible.

One last note about topic: I know a lot of them are dull. I tell students their task is to somehow work magic on it. I ask them to consider it a game. Take the dullest topic—paint drying, for instance—and make it exciting somehow. We will sometimes do this as a writing exercise. I tell them about the test of a real comedian: can they make reading out of the phone book funny? Viewing it as a game also takes some of the pressure off.

Real Writing Applications: Being able to focus a topic is an important writing skill. Many student writers will either have too broad a focus ("My Day at Disneyland!" turns into a list of rides with no details.) or too narrow a focus ("How I Pulled My Last Baby Tooth" can quickly run out of steam.) Also, although I tell them they should argue for the side they really believe in when they write for real audiences, they should always be capable of explaining the opposing sides arguments, of seeing both sides of the issue.

PROMPTED WRITING AND TIMED WRITING

I do some writing prompts during the year so that my students are used to the circumstances and timing of the test. I used to schedule a handful of them from the beginning of the school year through the week before the test. My district now requires three standard prompts to be administered during the school year, so I no longer add any myself for the most part—I just assign the district prompts. I do, however, give some practice with prompts throughout the year as Flash Nonfiction exercises. Timed writing prompts should never be the backbone of the writing curriculum, though I fear they may be in many schools. I use them mainly as writing "sketches."

Quick Outlines

Rather than making students write whole essays to prompts all the time, we practice brainstorming and outlining skills using prompts. I put a topic on the board, and students take a few minutes to brainstorm and then order their ideas. They get all the thought work of constructing a complete essay without the time and effort of having to actually do the writing. See Chapter 3, Content Dictates Form, for ideas about brainstorming and outlining.

Quick Paragraph Writing

I will sometimes open class with a quick paragraph writing assignment, or give it for homework. Sometimes I'll ask students to take one supporting paragraph idea from a prompt-inspired outline we've just done and actually develop it into a full paragraph, emphasizing specific details and word pictures. Again, students get practice writing to a prompt without all the work of writing the full essay. See Chapter 4, Picture This! for more about using details.

Timed Writing

On the occasions that I choose to give, or am required to give, timed writing prompts for a full essay, I try to create a situation as close to the actual test as possible. The Florida test is 45 minutes, as is my class. On the day I give a timed writing, I hand out photocopies of the state "planning" and "essay" papers. They will be used to show exactly how much space students will have on the real test. I hand out the prompt quickly, or put it on the board, and then give them as close to 45 minutes to write as possible. Once I collect the papers, however, I want the whole process to be more than "assign and assess."

Peer and Teacher Scoring

Very seldom will I simply take student prompts and assign them a score and hand them back. I usually give them back to students before I've even looked at them, so they can peer score. We do peer scoring in a variety of ways.

Exchanging Papers

1. Pair Share: I simply give the papers back to students who wrote them and have them pair up with someone for peer scoring.

2. Group Share: Sometimes I assign groups, hand back papers to the people who wrote them, and let them analyze the paper within the group.

3. Anonymous share: I ask students to put roster numbers from my attendance book onto their papers instead of their names, and I hand them out at random for pairs or groups to score. Sometimes I will exchange papers anonymously across classes.

Scoring Papers

Once students have learned to score the papers, this is fairly straightforward. They read the paper and assign it a score, in our case 1 through 6. I emphasize that these grades do not go into the grade book—only my score counts for the grade. The peer scores are merely a chance to evaluate each other's writing.

If I want the feedback to be a little more specific, I then ask students to analyze or rate the paper according to the traits included in the state rubric, sometimes on a chart like the one in Figure 11.1, where they can circle the score and comment.

FOCUS SCORE	ORGANIZATION SCORE	SUPPORT SCORE	CONVENTIONS SCORE	OVERALL SCORE
6 5 4 3 2 1	6 5 4 3 2 1	6 5 4 3 2 1	6 5 4 3 2 1	6 5 4 3 2 1
COMMENTS	COMMENTS	COMMENTS	COMMENTS	COMMENTS

Figure 11.1

Commenting on Papers

The chart raises the issue of commenting on each other's papers. This can be a sticky issue. I always strive to create a caring, safe environment in my classroom, where people can constructively criticize each other with carefully chosen, noninsulting words. I know from experience, however, that some middle school students are quite good at destructively criticizing each other with carelessly chosen, highly insulting words. Given this tendency, I often give students the following menu of comments to use. I tell them the menu gives them a general idea of the kinds of comments they should be making, but that they obviously can add other comments where they deem them necessary.

Use these comments on papers you peer score. Be diplomatic!

FEEDBACK

Good . . .

- prewrite
- organization—each paragraph was focused
- grabber—the 1st sentence got my attention
- clincher—it left me thinking
- specific details
- word pictures
- metaphors/similes

- hyperbole (overstatement for effect)
- sensory detail (sound, sight, smell, touch, and so on)
- sentence variety – this really flowed
- clear sentences
- word choices, especially _____
- use of strong verbs
- proofreading: hardly any mistakes!

SUGGESTIONS

Try to...

- create a prewrite, outline or web.
- separate into multiple paragraphs, one for each supporting idea.
- be sure your prewrite ideas are not too vague or too much alike.
- use a grabber that really gets our attention.
- end with a clincher that leaves us thinking.
- avoid endings like, "That's all I have to say," or anything close.
- be sure to create word pictures for your readers: specific images.
- make sure your details are not vague: "There was stuff everywhere."
- use sensory detail to show us sights, sounds, smells, and sensations.
- use some figurative language: metaphors, similes, and hyperbole.
- look at different aspects of a topic to get more details.

- look out for awkward "clunker sentences" that don't read smoothly.
- avoid sentences with unclear or multiple meanings.
- watch out for run-ons that use "and then" all the time.
- avoid using impressive vocabulary incorrectly.
- avoid using vague words like *nice, cool,* or *good.*
- avoid too much slang, especially inappropriate slang.
- use interesting words when you are sure of them and know their meaning.
- avoid run-ons.
- avoid fragments.
- be careful with commonly confused words: *it's/its, there/their/they're, your/you're*
- go over spelling in general more carefully.

Other Kinds of Feedback

In addition to scoring the papers, I will often ask my students to engage in other kinds of feedback that they are already adept at using from our "real" writing exercises.

Highlighters

Yes, it's highlighters again. The key to good writing (and high scores) is the number of specific details and word pictures, so I will often bring out the highlighters and ask students to mark up each other's papers. Highlighting all the specific details is a great way to get them see how much of the paper is specific and how much is vague. Most of the paper should be highlighted if they've written with enough specificity.

You can ask students to highlight nearly anything you are particularly looking for: good word choices, strong verbs, concrete nouns, good transitions, or figurative language.

Checking Organization

I will ask students to outline each other's papers, listing the main ideas for each paragraph. They should be able to see the flow of ideas pretty clearly. When writers get their papers back, they can compare their outline to the outline peers made. The closer they match up, the better the writer did at getting the overall ideas across.

Checking Proofreading

Students are writing a rough draft when they write for most standardized tests, but conventions and correctness still play a part in most rubrics. Having students spot-check each other for errors may help strengthen both the writer's and the peer reader's proofreading skills.

Teacher Feedback

There are easy ways for a teacher to give feedback on a prompt aside from just slapping a score on it. Any of the techniques I just listed above can be used by teachers as well, and coupled with personal feedback. Sometimes I add to the feedback students have already received from peers.

USING TIME WELL

As I noted earlier, students in Florida get exactly 45 minutes to read the prompt, interpret the prompt, prewrite, write, and proofread their essays. That isn't much time. I give my students a rough breakdown of how they might best use their time.

Prompt and Prewrite

I tell students that they should take a minute or two to read the prompt, then three or four to do their prewrite. If they take more than that, they lose too much actual writing time; if they take less, they may misinterpret the prompt or skimp on structuring their essay well.

Introduction

An effective introduction pulls the reader in and sets the tone for the essay. I advise students to keep it as short and punchy as possible. The introduction needs to grab the reader's attention, and it usually needs to get the main idea out (but not always). It does not need to state all the supporting ideas in advance of actually talking about them, though some writers feel more comfortable doing so. I tell them to get the introduction over with fast and move into the heart of the paper.

Body

The body of the paper is the middle paragraphs—and there are not necessarily three of them. Since my students only have two pages to work with, I tell them they have a range of reasons (middle paragraphs) to work with. They need at least two, or there's not much sign of thought going on. I have seen a four-paragraph essay receive top marks. Depending on how small they write, students might even be able to squeeze in five reasons to create a seven-paragraph essay. Five paragraphs are okay, too, if that is the number needed. I emphasize that they are not just throwing up any three reasons that come into their heads in no particular order. Like any essay, content dictates form.

I emphasize that this is the main part of their paper, the one that will make or break it score-wise—and that it's all about the pictures, the pictures, THE PICTURES! I tell students they should be wrapping up the body of their paper about 35 minutes into the test. That will leave them about ten minutes to write a clincher that wraps up their piece.

Clincher

I review the requirements for a good clincher (conclusion), and encourage students to come up with the best clincher they can on short notice. I think clinchers are even harder to come up with than grabbers, but equally important. I tell them that under no circumstances should they end the paper with "That's all I have to say," "That was my paper. I hope you liked it," or "Bye-bye." By the time we're to the test, though, that usually goes without saying, except as a joke.

Looking Over Your Draft

For the last five minutes—or however long they have left—I tell students to quickly look over their paper for any errors, especially missing words, misspellings, and run-ons and fragments. I tell them to keep looking over their papers till time is called.

WOW THE SCORERS

Lastly, at some point near the test day, I tell them to picture the poor, poor souls assigned to score standardized writing tests. They read paper after paper for days on end, paper after paper on the same, dull topic. I ask my students to think about how many of the essays sound exactly the same, how many of them are dull, formulaic, and without distinctive detail or any sense of a real person writing them. I tell them to have mercy on these poor souls.

I ask them to imagine reading paper after paper about the best friend who is "funny, fun, and friendly." Paper after paper about the vacation trip that is "fun and really cool." Paper after paper about how "gum tastes good and helps us think."

I ask them to imagine getting their own paper. It brims with delicious detail. It doesn't follow the formula, yet it is intelligently, even elegantly, organized. In fact, it doesn't quite sound like the work of a student. It sounds like the work of a . . . real writer.

Perhaps it is an urban myth, but I have been told that when such a paper crosses the path of one of our poor, hapless scorers, they have been known to stand on a chair and yell, "I've got a live one!"

I tell students I want them to be "live ones."

More importantly, I tell them that hapless, anonymous scorers are not their chief audience. The real final result of a good writing class is not found in a test score, but in communicating real ideas for a real purpose—and reaching real people. Achieving this end—actual communication with other people—is the subject of our final chapter.

CHAPTER 12

Real Writers: Publishing and Printing

Let me begin the end of this book with a worst-case scenario. It is a scenario you may be playing out in your own classroom right now, probably without anyone thinking less of you for it. It is a scenario I end up acting out in my classroom more often than I would like. It is the scenario that our current "initiatives" and push for "rigor" have forced many of us play out.

Here is the scenario. Students write to ready-made prompts, not because they have something to say but because we tell them to say something. They write for an audience of one—the teacher—not anyone they really want to communicate with. Students write to meet the requirements of a prefabricated rubric, not so much to meet the complicated requirements of reaching a real audience. They receive all their feedback from the teacher, which pretty much amounts to a score on the rubric scale. "You wrote a 4. Congratulations." The result of all their hard work is that this writing goes into their writing portfolio, which is later passed on to the high school teacher who doesn't have time to look at it; or, if the writing folder doesn't get passed on, the writing leaves your room to begin a journey toward home, only to be trashed somewhere along the way.

Students trash their writing because it doesn't mean anything to them.

By asking us to teach to a standardized writing test, the Powers That Be are asking us to create writing that is artificial from beginning to end. Real writers don't write to prompts (at least not ones that are forced upon them). Real writers write to the demands of a particular genre or publication, but never to a one-size-fits-all formula. Real writers don't write for an audience of one or two people whose only function in reading their work is to score it. Real writers may write for their own purposes, or to meet a set of professional guidelines. Technical writers and newspaper writers, for example, follow guidelines that tell them what to include, how to organize their information, and what stylistic features are acceptable. But they realize that those guidelines are for that particular kind of writing—the guidelines are not an all-encompassing rubric that applies to all types of writing. Real writers don't write so they can get a score, and then file and later throw out their writing. The whole structure has become artificial from beginning to end—because we have allowed it.

Granted, school is a somewhat artificial environment. Many, if not most, of our students might never write if we didn't "make them." But school is an artificial environment that is designed to get them ready for the real world—not for another artificial environment. We should be training our students to act like real writers, not to simply pass "the test."

In his essay from *The Right Words at the Right Time*, Jay Leno talks about how much the book *Mike Mulligan and His Steam Shovel* meant to him. He, like the characters in the book, always did better "when someone was watching." I think we're all like that, to a certain extent, and our students are no different. You write differently when you are writing for a real audience. But how to find an audience? It can be surprisingly easy if you make it a priority.

Low-Tech Publishing

When I was in seventh grade, our class wrote very short science-fiction stories based on a one-sentence story-starter. The very next day my teacher, Mrs. Bronson, handed out dittos (remember dittos?) to the whole class. She had typed up my version of the story and made copies. She proceeded to read the story to the entire class and extol its virtues. I will admit that I have long since lost the actual story, but I never forgot the experience. It didn't matter that the audience was small or the fame fleeting. My writing had been published!

Publishing does not have to be high-tech, and the pieces published do not have to be long. As I mentioned back in Chapter 4, publishing can be as simple as taking a single good sentence, putting it on a poster, and posting it somewhere in the school. Even if you don't have easy computer access for your students, writing things out neatly by hand still has some uses in the world. (I teach my students the art of the hand-written thank-you note when we have guest speakers.)

If a student has written an excellent essay, create a spot on the wall to post it in your room. Or in the media center. Or in the cafeteria. By the front office, near the gym, out by parent pick-up. Having student work on display around the school helps create a more "literate" atmosphere in a school.

Mid-Tech Publishing

The technology available at a given school and within a particular school population varies widely. My middle school is fortunate in many respects; we are small school, with a population of about 750 students, and we have two full computer labs, so scheduling time in a lab can be complicated at times but not impossible. I know that at some of the larger middle schools in my district, with populations of around 3,000, getting time in a computer lab can be virtually impossible.

We are additionally fortunate at our school to be the beneficiaries of a technology grant that gave us five carts of Alphasmart 3000's. Each cart has 30 Alphasmarts, a class set of little word processors students can use to draft and print their drafts for revision right in my classroom without the need to try to get the computer lab reserved for days on end. Once they have finished drafting, I can upload the drafts through the cart into my computer, and from there place them on the shared drive in our computer lab. Students can then add their revisions and proofread in Microsoft Word.

Another huge benefit I have in my district is a centralized copy center. I can take any document I create on my computer and send it directly to the copy center online with instructions for page setup and binding. The copies are then delivered to school.

The other variable involved in technology is what students themselves bring to the table. Many of my students have both home computers and flash drives, which gives them a way to finish pieces at home if they are absent or can't quite finish a particular piece in the allotted time at school.

I share the particulars of my school's technology situation because they have helped shape how I deal with student publishing. You may have a lot less to work with—you may have a lot more. But no matter what level of technology you have available, you always have some options.

Creating Anthologies

When I started teaching, school computer labs, and even home computers, were just coming into play. If you wanted to publish anything, you either had to type it yourself, or beg your students to somehow get it typed. If you have no lab at your school, or a lab with very limited availability, then you are in the same situation. If publishing is a priority, though, you can ask students to type their pieces at home and bring them to you.

Assuming that you have some kind of technology available for your students to type their pieces, assembling an anthology is fairly easy, but not if you do it the old-fashioned way. The old-fashioned way is to have students give you their hard copies, which you assemble into a booklet to be copied. There are many drawbacks to this method. If you find additional mistakes in a hard copy, they are very awkward to correct—you end up using correction fluid and hand-printing to fix a printed copy. Students will bring you essays of widely varying quality in other ways, as well: crumpled papers, strange fonts, weird colors of ink, and documents printed on a cartridge's last legs. The stack of papers you end up with may not be suitable for running through your copy machine or sending to a copy center.

It's far better to assemble an anthology digitally, and these days there are multiple ways to get the job done.

If you have computer lab at school, see if you have a shared drive that can be accessed from any computer in the lab. Our lab has an "H" drive with a "Students" folder. Within this folder I have my own folder, and within that folder, a folder for each class and a "Publish" folder. I have access to every student's file, and when they tell me they are ready to publish, I give each paper a last look-over for any glaring mistakes, and then tell the author to save it to the "Publish" folder. I then take any documents that are in the "Publish" folder and copy and paste them into one large document. Once I've assembled the anthology into one document, I have control of fonts, editing, and page set up. It only takes a minute to send the whole booklet to the copy center online.

If you don't have access to the computer lab, or if some students need to finish their essays at home, there are other ways to get the essays assembled into a booklet on your computer. My students all have my school e-mail address, and they can e-mail their essays as attachments. They can also bring them in on a computer disk, CD, or flash drive for me to upload.

If you don't have a copy center, you may be able to make the copies yourself on your school copier—depending on how well it works. If administrators object to this use of the copier, I would point out how important publishing can be in improving student writing. If this doesn't convince them, tell them publishing student writing will raise test scores. This nearly always works. But seriously, if you do not have unlimited copies at your disposal, there are other options. Ask your PTA to help out with publishing costs. Write a letter to parents asking for their assistance. Who knows? Maybe one of them owns a Kinko's franchise! In my district we have an organization called FUTURES, which supplies mini-grants to teachers. Look for both local and state grant opportunities to help you in your efforts to publish.

There are different formats you can use to publish student anthologies once they are assembled. When I taught seventh grade language arts all day, I would assemble one big anthology with at least one piece from nearly all of my 150 students and then distribute a copy to every student and to administrators and other teachers. Another option is to create a smaller anthology for each class, with first period getting its own booklet, and second, and third, and so on.

If you are severely limited on copy numbers, another option is to print a limited number to have in class, and then make the computer file available to students if they'd like to take it home and print it themselves. I have also assembled pieces and then saved them to CD's for students to take home and either print or view on their computers.

Assuming you are making copies, though—what do you do with them? I sometimes distribute them to every student, and the day I hand out those booklets is very exciting. Usually the whole class period is spent simply reading the booklets and enjoying them. Most students will have read a few of the pieces during conferences, but for the most part, the booklet is all new material for them. I also save booklets and keep them in my room for future students to look at. Students love to look at booklets from past years—they can critique them, get ideas from them, and simply enjoy them. Seeing other students' work published can also inspire them to want to be published. I usually put a few in the front office, student services, and the media center for other students and for school visitors to read. If you have done a permission-to-publish form (see Appendix B) for parents to sign, and they are aware that the writing may be seen beyond the school setting, asking local businesses (especially businesses of parents) to put some copies of your anthology in their waiting rooms can help get student writing "out there." You can even put your teacher e-mail address on the booklet, so readers can e-mail comments to you to share with students. Another option, depending on the type of anthology, is to share copies of more "upbeat" writing with senior centers or nursing homes. You can even do a "large-print" edition by changing the font size!

Writing Contests

I am not going to attempt a comprehensive list of student writing contests. They are out there. I did a search for "student essay writing contests" online just now, and there were 577,000 returns ("student writing contests," without the essay, yielded 3,700,000 entries). Many of the essays come with cash prizes, savings bonds, or scholarships. Some of them get published in magazines or newspapers. I try to call my students' attention to as many contests as I can, though I tend to avoid contests that require an entry fee. For the most part, students need to enter these contests on their own, so aside from possibly helping students get their essays ready, you have very little work to do.

Real Writing Situations

There are a number of places for students to get published that do not involve a contest at all. They can write letters to the editor or submit editorial commentary like the "My Word" essays I write for the *Orlando Sentinel*. They can write essays or articles for organizational newsletters: religious organizations, scouts, service clubs, and so on. They can write for the school newspaper. They can write letters to magazines they read. Encourage them to bring school-appropriate magazines to class one day and take a look at the "mailbox" sections at the front. Students read everything from *People* to *Thrasher* to *Discover*, and all of those magazines offer forums for students to voice their opinions.

High-Tech Publishing

High-tech doesn't have to be high-stress. There are safe, stress-free ways to get student writing online and in print with the use of the computer. Here are three of the best ways to put technology to use.

Publishing Online

The chief resistance I have run into with "public" online publishing is the fear that putting student work online will attract unwanted attention and put students at some kind of risk. I have been discouraged from publishing this way in my county due to that concern.

I am loath to publish a list of available Web sites that publish student work, due to the ever changing nature of the Internet. What I publish as a great site now might vanish next week. On top of that factor, each of these sites has its own unique way of operating—to try to describe them all would be overwhelming. There are sites out there, though. *Teen Ink* has been around for nineteen years and publishes both online and in print. Do an online search for "student publishing" and see what you get. There are sites that accept student work for online publishing at their site, as well as sites that enable you to set up your own publishing pages. There are too many possibilities to discuss in depth here—but they are worth looking into.

Wikis

Another option for publishing online that avoids exposing students to the general public is to create a wiki. A wiki is place where writers can publish their writing, and then get feedback on it, during the revision process, or after the piece is finalized, or both.

At WikiSpaces.com, you can set up a free wiki page for each of your students, each with a private password. This password enables students to post their essays on their pages. Then other students in the class can visit the site using their passwords and make comments on each other's writing. As the teacher, you can monitor all communications between students and make sure that they are all appropriate. If you have any tech-savvy teachers at your school, they can help you. I had help from two other teachers in setting up my Wikispace and then introducing it to students. I only learned about wikis recently (and their connection to Wikipedia), and started using them even more recently, but I'll have to say I'm hooked. They are useful for publishing, but also at other, earlier stages of the writing process, such as conferencing.

Recently my students typed rough drafts of "Right Words at the Right Time" essays and saved them on the media center computer shared drive. I gave each of my students their user names and passwords to my Wikispace on little slips of paper and let them log on. They copied and pasted their essays onto their own main pages, then clicked on discussions. Within minutes students were reading one another's rough essays online, and then posting responses to give feedback. Instead of the usual conference with feedback from one person, or maybe three in a small group, they were getting feedback from five to ten people in 20 minutes. As with written conferences, I set rules about how to phrase suggestions and feedback, and I also enforce a "no-instant-messaging-speak rule." They must write their online messages in complete sentences.

Students can use rough-draft feedback as they see fit, and revise their papers right at their Wikispace from home. I can leave them comments as well. Using my Wikispace may change the way I handle my own feedback and proofreading of student essays. It will give me a chance to read and respond to their papers while they are still working on them, and without having to collect the papers, which interrupts their writing process.

When the writing process is over, then students can publish on their space and get feedback on their finished product as well. Although this writing will not be available to the general public, it is available for all students in all your classes, thus creating a much wider audience than just the few students in a small group in a single period. And the chance to see each other's writing online and make comments there is very attractive to most students. The fact that the space is private means that the security issues parents worry about at a public site are nonexistent. Also, since you can monitor all of their messages, there is minimal chance of any inappropriate online behavior within the class. The "start-up"—which includes setting up your space and typing and submitting user-names and passwords for all your classes—takes a little time, but is well worth the effort.

The first time I had students conferencing on the Wikispace, they groaned when the bell rang at the end of class. They were having too much fun reading each other's essays. They didn't want class to be over. How often does that happen with middle schoolers?

Web Self-Publishing

If you wanted to create a really nice collection of student writing, one place to do it is lulu.com; another is wordclay.com. Wordclay enables you to upload any kind of book—poetry collections, novels, plays, or essay collections—to their Web site. They will create it as a real, bound and published paperback book with an ISBN. This is then available online for sale—but is only printed on an as-needed basis. The books can be made available only to the author, or to the general public, and they can be downloaded as e-books as well as published on paper and mailed. One family at our school wrote a young adult novel together, *$200 Worth of Trouble*, and has had a wonderful time publishing it, promoting it, and selling it.

BEST-CASE SCENARIO

I began this chapter with a worst-case scenario where students write only for the test, which becomes their (and our) only measure of success. So what is the best-case scenario, the type of writing we should be shooting for?

In my best-case scenario, our students are engaged in their own lives, and in the world around them (writing can help encourage both types of engagement), so they have things to write about that are important to them—and to those around them. Our students know how to structure their writing based on their audience and topic. Our students know how to write with detail, logic, and grace. They revise their papers with care because they know their writing is going somewhere—before a real audience. When their papers are done, they are read not just by the teacher, but by as many people as possible. Their primary motivator is not a score or grade, but the pleasure of having reached an audience.

As a fan of the Stephen Covey book *The Seven Habits of Highly Effective People* (pretentious title; great book), I try to keep the "second habit" in mind when I work with my students: Begin with the end in mind.

If our end is passing test scores, we may get them, but not much else. If our end is to create real writers, we can have outstanding test scores, and a whole lot more thrown in.

It is easy to dread grading essays when they are meaningless exercises in formulaic writing. I've done it myself—stared at the stack for longer and longer periods of time, growing more and more intimidated by them.

But it doesn't have to be that way.

As time goes by, I have actually started looking forward to that stack of papers, not so much because I have to grade it, but because the essays are so much fun, so moving, so real—they are a pleasure to read. What more could anyone wish for?

WAYS TO ORGANIZE AN ESSAY

Order of Importance or Stand-up Comedy Order
(Put your second-best reason first, and then build to your best reason.)

Chronological Order
(Tell things in time order—from beginning to end!)

Circular Chronological Order
(Begin at the end, then circle through the story back to the end again.)

Chronological With Insights
(Tell a story—but make points along the way.)

Spatial Order
(Talk about a space or a place—up/down, left/right, near/far.)

Cause and Effect Order
(A causes B, which causes C, which causes . . .)

Affected People
(Discuss each group your issue will affect: students, teachers, parents, animals, clowns. . . .)

Problem/Solution
(Tell what the problem is, then present a solution and explain why it will work.)

Compare/Contrast
Comparison: Topic One, Topic Two
Comparison: Point by Point
Comparison: Similarities and Differences

Geometric Logic
(If A is true, then B is true. If B is true, then C is true . . .)

End Reveal or Main-Idea-at-the-End
(Open up with the issues, but don't reveal your point of view until the end.)

The Turn-About Essay
(Knock down the opposing argument, step by step.)

APPENDIX B

PERMISSION-TO-PUBLISH FORM

I acknowledge that my student, _____,

is planning to publish the following piece(s) in a printed anthology for Mr. Finkle's class:

_____

_____

_____

_____

I understand that this anthology booklet will be distributed to Mr. Finkle's 8th grade class, put in the Media Center and front office, and kept in Mr. Finkle's room for current and future students to read. I also understand that my student will receive extra credit for each piece that Mr. Finkle agrees to publish.

Signed _____ (Parent)

"Neat People vs. Sloppy People"

BY SUZANNE BRITT

I've finally figured out the difference between neat people and sloppy people. The distinction is, as always, moral. Neat people are lazier and meaner than sloppy people.

Sloppy people, you see, are not really sloppy. Their sloppiness is merely the unfortunate consequence of their extreme moral rectitude. Sloppy people carry in their mind's eye a heavenly vision, a precise plan, that is so stupendous, so perfect, it can't be achieved in this world or the next.

Sloppy people live in Never-Never Land. Someday is their metier. Someday they are planning to alphabetize all their books and set up home catalogs. Someday they will go through their wardrobes and mark certain items for tentative mending and certain items for passing on to relatives of similar shape and size. Someday sloppy people will make family scrapbooks into which they will put newspaper clippings, postcards, locks of hair, and the dried corsage from their senior prom. Someday they will file everything on the surface of their desks, including the cash receipts from coffee purchases at the snack shop. Someday they will sit down and read all the back issues of *The New Yorker*.

For all these noble reasons and more, sloppy people never get neat. They aim too high and wide. They save everything, planning someday to file, order, and straighten out the world. But while these ambitious plans take clearer and clearer shape in their heads, the books spill from the shelves onto the floor, the clothes pile up in the hamper and closet, the family mementos accumulate in every drawer, the surface of the desk is buried under mounds of paper, and the unread magazines threaten to reach the ceiling.

Sloppy people can't bear to part with anything. They give loving attention to every detail. When sloppy people say they're going to tackle the surface of a desk, they really mean it. Not a paper will go unturned; not a rubber band will go unboxed. Four hours or two weeks into the excavation, the desk looks exactly the same, primarily because the sloppy person is meticulously creating new piles of papers with new headings and scrupulously stopping to read all the old book catalogs before he throws them away. A neat person would just bulldoze the desk.

Neat people are bums and clods at heart. They have cavalier attitudes toward possessions, including family heirlooms. Everything is just another dust-catcher to them. If anything collects dust, it's got to go and that's that. Neat people will toy with the idea of throwing the children out of the house just to cut down on the clutter. Neat people don't care about process. They like results. What they want to do is get the whole thing over with so they can sit down and watch the rasslin' on TV. Neat people operate on two unvarying principles: Never handle any item twice and throw everything away.

The only thing messy in a neat person's house is the trash can. The minute something comes to a neat person's hand, he will look at it, try to decide if it has immediate use and, finding none, throw it in the trash.

Neat people are especially vicious with mail. They never go through that mail unless they are standing directly over a trash can. If the trash can is beside the mailbox, even better. All ads, catalogs, pleas for charitable contributions, church bulletins, and money-saving coupons go straight into the trash can without being opened. All letters from home, postcards from Europe, bills and paychecks are opened, immediately responded to, then dropped in the trash can. Neat people keep their receipts only for tax purposes. That's it. No sentimental salvaging of birthday cards or the last letter a dying relative ever wrote. Into the trash it goes.

Neat people place neatness above everything, even economics. They are incredibly wasteful. Neat people throw away several toys every time they walk through the den. I knew a neat person once who threw away a perfectly good dish drainer because it had mold on it. The drainer was too much trouble to wash. And neat people will sell their furniture when they move. They will sell a La-Z-Boy recliner while you are reclining in it.

Neat people are no good to borrow from. Neat people buy everything in expensive little single portions. They get their flour and sugar in two-pound bags. They wouldn't consider clipping a coupon, saving a leftover, reusing plastic nondairy-whipped-cream containers, or rinsing off tin foil and draping it over the unmoldy dish drainer. You can never borrow a neat person's newspaper to see what's playing at the movies. Neat people have the paper all wadded up and in the trash by 7:05 AM.

Neat people cut a clean swath through the organic as well as the inorganic world. People, animals, and things are all one to them. They are so insensitive. After they've finished with the pantry, the medicine cabinet, and the attic, they throw out the red geranium (too many leaves), sell the dog (too many fleas), and send the children off to boarding school (too many scuff marks on the hardwood floors).

This essay is from a book of essays called *Show and Tell* that was published in 1983. Suzanne has another book of essays called *Skinny People Are Dull and Crunchy Like Carrots,* which was published in 1982.

REFERENCES

Barry, D. (1994). *The world according to Dave Barry*. New York: Random House.

Blumner, R. (2007, April 1). Denying overtime akin to slavery. *St. Petersburg Times*, p. 5P.

Broder, D. (2007, April 10). Time for a bargain on the war. *Washington Post*, p. A17.

Cameron, J. (2002). *The artist's way*. New York: Jeremy P. Tarcher/Putnam.

Cameron, J. (1999). *The right to write: An invitation and initiation into the writing life*. New York: Jeremy P. Tarcher/Putnam.

Covey, S. (1990). *The seven habits of highly effective people*. New York: Free Press.

Diaz, G. (2007, April 1.) Fire, brimstone Crossley now preaches ACLU purity. *Orlando Sentinel. P. A23.*

Finkle, D. (2007, February 11). How I help my students break out of the FCAT Writing cage. *Orlando Sentinel*. J7 Volusia edition.

Fulghum, R. (2004). *All I really need to know I learned in kindergarten* (rev. ed.). New York: Ballantine.

Fulghum, R. (1997). *Uh-Oh: Some observations from both sides of the refrigerator door*. New York: Ballantine.

Fulghum, R. (1995). *Maybe (maybe not): Second thoughts from a secret life*. New York: Ivy Books.

Fulghum, R. (1991). *It was on fire when I lay down on it*. New York: Ivy Books.

Lane, M. (2006, February 8). Lincoln's lowly FCAT scores. *Daytona Beach News-Journal*, p. 1C.

Lanza, R. (2007, Spring). A new theory of the universe. *American Scholar*. Retrieved March 10, 2008, from http://www.theamericanscholar.org/archives/sp07/newtheory-lanza.html.

Lewis, C. S. (1970). *God in the dock: Essays on theology and ethics*. Grand Rapids, MI: Wm. B. Eerdmans.

King, S. (2000). *On writing: A memoir of the craft*. New York: Scribner.

Parker, K. (2007, April 1). Killing cartoons into submission. *Orlando Sentinel*.

Roessing, L. (2004). Toppling the idol. *English Journal, 94*(1), 41–46.

Sagan, C. (1985). *Cosmos*. New York: Ballantine.

Smith, M. W., & Wilhelm, J. (2007). *Getting it right: Fresh approaches to teaching grammar, usage, and correctness*. New York: Scholastic.

Thomas, M. compiler. (2002). *The right words at the right time*. New York: Atria.

Watford, Bels. (2006). *$200 worth of trouble*. Retrieved March 11, 2008, from http://www.lulu.com/content/372769.

Wilhelm, J. (2001). *Using think-aloud strategies to improve reading comprehension*. New York: Scholastic.

Wilson, M. (2006). *Rethinking rubrics in writing assessment*. Portsmouth, NH: Heinemann.

BIBLIOGRAPHY

Allison, J, & Gediman, G. D. (Eds.). (2007). *This I believe: The personal philosophies of remarkable men and women*. New York: Holt Paperbacks.

Aurandt, P. (1984). *Paul Harvey's the rest of the story*. New York: Bantam.

Baggini, J. (2006). *The pig who wants to be eaten: 100 experiments for the armchair philosopher*. New York: Plume.

Friedman, T. L. (2007). *The world is flat: A brief history of the twenty-first century*. New York: Picador.

Grodin, C., compiler. (2007). *If I only knew then . . . learning from our mistakes*. New York: Springboard Press.

Quindlen, A. (1989). *Living out loud*. New York: Ivy Books.

Thomas, M. (2004, November 11). Just hang up and drive—it's a lifesaver. *Orlando Sentinel*.